Advanced Praise for A Little Birdie Told Me...

"This inspiring book has something for everyone. Matt has masterfully and seamlessly weaved his story into life lessons, some provided from the difficult part of his journey. *A Little Birdie Told Me...* will resonate with bird lovers, baseball fans, and all those in between."

*— **Tim Kurkjian**, New York Times Best-Selling Author and Major League Baseball Analyst for ESPN*

"*A Little Birdie Told Me...* is a book that offers inspiration and valuable learnings for all readers, including business leaders and those who want to become a more empathetic and understanding executive. The lessons Matthew shares during his journey of self-reflection are relatable and applicable to all of us and I recommend this book to fellow hoteliers, parents, and citizens of the world."

*— **Hervé J.L. Humler**, Chairman Emeritus, The Ritz-Carlton Hotel Company*

"A delightful read — Matt has such an easy way with words. He skillfully weaves important life lessons around his newfound passion for birds, discovered during the pandemic lockdown. We can all relate to the wise lessons in this book and laugh at some of the amusing experiences Matt shared. By the end of this book, you will feel like you and Matt are old friends."

*— **Peter G. Kaestner**, World's No. 1 eBirder with 9,294 Species Observed*

"*A Little Birdie Told Me...* is an absorbing set of life lessons forged from a journey through nature and self-reflection. Whether in crisis or calm, this book demonstrates the power of being more fully attendant to naturally occurring beauty, tranquility, and majesty. If you're ready to venture down an insightful path to peace, purposefulness, and success, it's time to step into this book."

– *Joseph Michelli*, *PhD, New York Times No. 1 Best-Selling author of books like Stronger Through Adversity, The Airbnb Way, and Leading the Starbucks Way*

"*A Little Birdie Told Me...* is not about COVID, losing your job, or birding. COVID offers context, job loss represents the unexpected challenges life can throw at any of us, and birding illustrates how being receptive to the wonders of the world can enrich our lives and feed our souls. The narrative is honest, vulnerable, and inspiring. Papuchis is masterful at inviting readers to embrace the work on their terms. His approach is consistent with the sentiment expressed by Kahlil Gibran's famous quote: "If he is indeed wise, he does not bid you enter the house of his wisdom, but rather leads you to the threshold of your mind." Enjoy this wonderful read and buy a copy for someone you love."

– *Leo Bottary,* *author of three books, including Peennovation: What Peer Advisory Groups Can Teach Us About Building High-Performing Teams*

A LITTLE BIRDIE TOLD ME...

*A Journey to Find Hope,
Happiness and the Wings to Fly*

MATTHEW PAPUCHIS

A LITTLE BIRDIE TOLD ME...

Cover Design by Juan Pablo Ruiz
Layout by Manuel Serna

Printed in the United States of America

For more information, contact:
Fig Factor Media, LLC | www.figfactormedia.com

ISBN: 978-1-952779-86-2
Library of Congress Number: 2021905561

To Kristie, for giving me the time, space, and support to take this journey.

To Dylan, Noah, and Emma, for providing me countless moments of inspiration and pride as I've watched you find your wings, which will not only help you fly but soar.

TABLE OF CONTENTS

PREFACE

A Birding Book That's Not Just About Birds

Welcome. Before you get too far, there is something you should know. This book isn't necessarily about birds, birding, or bird photography, per se. Yes, this book covers those things, but it isn't about them specifically. It is, to an extent, in that birding and bird photography became the vehicle by which I embarked upon a journey of self-discovery and reflection to find hope and happiness during the spring and summer of 2020 as I struggled to come to grips with, and accept, being out of work for the first time since I was 14 years old.

That's 26 years, for the record. Like many in my industry, my career was put on hold when my position at global hotel company, Marriott International, was eliminated, due to lack of travel demand because of the COVID-19 pandemic. And, as I found myself—for the first time in a quarter century—searching for something to cling to for hope, I was able to find that in, of all things, birds. The birds who have been around me for years, but I never took the time to hear what they had to say. Until I finally gave myself the permission to stop and listen.

Nevertheless, this book isn't designed, nor is it guaranteed, to help you become the world's foremost birdwatching expert.

Sure, I have some tips I've picked up since I joined the birding community, and they are included in here, but making you a better birder is not what this book is intended to do. Given that I began this hobby in May of 2020, I am hardly in a position to write such a book. Just to put it into perspective, the No. 1 eBirderin the world—in terms of overall number of species observed—is a gentleman named Peter Kaestner. As I type this, he has seen 9,261 different species of birds in his lifetime (out of an estimated 10,000 or so).

For the record, at the time I type this, I am ranked 93,461st with 115 observations. So, as the proudly ranked 93,000+th birder in the world, I am not deluded enough to think I am worthy of giving you a ton of advice on birding in and of itself. So, then, what exactly is this book about?

This book is about the journey I've been on since the spring of 2020 as I tried to stay positive and optimistic in the face of adversity and as I looked toward a future filled with uncertainty. And, even though I have written this book, and as of September 2020, rejoined the workforce, this journey is not yet complete. It never will be. But I felt now was the time to tell this story. When I finally went back to work last fall, a friend wrote to me and said, "I hope the writing continues…and the bird photos, too!" So, here it is.

Finding a passion for birds when I did, allowed me to

survive that unprecedented time. And I don't use that word *survive* lightly. It is not an exaggeration to say the birds saved my life. They definitely saved my spirit, my soul, and my sanity. They enabled me to find peace, find myself, and experience new joys during what was arguably the most challenging time of my life.

I also want to clarify I also would not have been able to get through the tough times without the love and support of my family. However, as grateful as I am to have such a close-knit and caring support network, and as much as I am blessed to have their unconditional support, they, unfortunately, were not able to help me find inner peace. Because no matter how many times my family told me they loved me or told me not to worry, none of that made much of a difference in terms of my psyche or when battling my own feelings of self-defeat.

For the most part, it would have to be up to me to come to terms with the reality of my situation, to find peace and comfort with the hand I was dealt, and then find positive ways to move forward and stay focused. At the end of the day, it is always up to us.

Despite knowing I was still blessed in many ways, during some of the more difficult days of unemployment, there were moments I felt like a failure for not being able to financially provide for my family in the same way I had since my oldest of three children was born in 2009. I've since come to accept, and even embrace, the fact I was able to provide for them and be there for them in a much different but equally important way—by having more time to create special memories and by being more available and present in their lives. And, of course, by sharing my new-found passion with my kids and exposing them to nearby parks and nature trails we never knew existed before last spring.

Dad's infamous "Field Trip Days" weren't always met with the biggest smiles, but I know they enjoyed the weekly excursions more than they let on, and I'm hopeful they will be appreciative as they get older. It took some time for me to reach this point of acceptance, but I got there. Again, thanks—in large part—to the birds.

At this point, you may be asking yourselves, "Did the birds really do *all* that? Help you find peace, solace, and perspective? Hope and happiness?" Like I said, sort of. By escaping and finding yourself lost, weaving in and out of wildlife preserves and nature trails in the hot Florida sun all summer, you have a lot of time to be alone with your thoughts as you wander in the sweltering heat. You have the opportunity to reflect. To gain clarity and perspective. To soul search. To soak it all in. To realize the world is much bigger than you thought. To heal. To talk to yourself (yes, I did that, and still do). To remind yourself what is important in life. And you get to do that while engaging in a challenging and rewarding activity that will push your boundaries as you explore a relatively unknown world.

So, yes, the birding—again, as a vehicle to achieve this sense of self-discovery—helped me do all those things these past few months. It provided lifelong lessons I will take with me forever; ones I can apply to both my personal and professional life. And *that* is what this book is about.

I have learned things that will serve me well in all future endeavors, whether at work or at home, or life in general. And, I have decided to turn those lessons into a book and share these valuable learnings with professionals and parents alike. Things such as positivity, perseverance, patience, perspective, and the importance of preparation. Each chapter is based on a specific experience or "aha moment" I had while engaging in birding and how the lesson applies beyond the confines of the birding world. Peppered throughout, I also share other personal stories from my life that help give you more insight into my journey, which give additional context to these lessons.

While I cannot guarantee you will become a better birder, I can say with confidence, you will be able to benefit from these lessons I learned while I canvased South Florida in search of those hidden gems and in search of myself. Perhaps, you will be inspired to venture out and try this activity yourself, to discover what the birds tell you. Either way, the lessons in the coming pages are designed to help you become a more understanding professional, parent, partner, and person.

INTRODUCTION

A Journey to Find Hope, Happiness, and the Wings to Fly

A quiet morning at the Plantation Preserve Linear Trail, Plantation, Florida—May 2020.

This is 2020. It just has an awesome ring to it, doesn't it? And, if you didn't read that in the voice of the famed news broadcaster, Barbara Walters, go back and read it again.

I, like most people one could assume, looked forward to 2020 with great anticipation. For one, it was the start of a new decade and for me personally, the year I was turning 40 years old (somehow), and it also marked the fortieth anniversary of the *Miracle on Ice.* This, of course, is the moniker given to the United States' infamous upset win over the Soviet Union at the 1980 Winter Olympics in Lake Placid, New York. On top of that, the term 2020 conjures images of perfection, as in a person with 20/20 vision.

So, how could it not be met with high hopes and optimism? But, as we found out less than three months into the year, what started as a year full of promise and possibility, quickly unraveled. I won't try to convince you my situation was unique, because in most ways, it wasn't. As shared in the preface, I was among the thousands across the hospitality sector—from airlines to cruise ships and theme parks to hotels—whose career was put on hold without so much as three weeks' warning, thanks to the immediate impact COVID-19 had on our business.

While I was not alone when that happened to me, there is one more thing to add. On Thursday, March 26, 2020, when I found out my role at Marriott International was eliminated due to contingency plans the company was forced to put in place, it was the second time that year I heard those words. About two months earlier, on January 31, 2020, to be exact, I received the news the position I had held for three years was eliminated, effective February 14. Yep, Valentine's Day. So, when I was able to land a job internally, within that two-week period, to stay with the company after all, well, I was more confident than ever about the future. I felt this new role was the start of something new. Something big.

I jumped on an airplane two weeks later for a quick trip to Marriott's headquarters in Bethesda, Maryland, for some meetings with my new team. While COVID-19 was obviously already on the radar screens of our company's senior executives for weeks if not months, especially since we have a large presence in China, it still hadn't entered the collective consciousness of most employees at my company, or anywhere else for that matter. Besides, I was too busy feeling great and patting myself on the back for surviving the job elimination just a couple of weeks prior. I flew back to South Florida on February 26, feeling as high as the jet I was on. Exactly one month later, I found out just how badly the pandemic was already wreaking havoc on our industry, and even worse, how much more it potentially could.

So, no, my situation was not *that* unique. Sure, it was tough coming to terms with the fact that, for the first time since I was

14, I wasn't earning a paycheck, but I was not alone. Clearly. And that did actually help in many ways—by adopting a "we're all in this together" mindset. But the added element of hearing those words once, then bouncing back and feeling great, only to have the rug pulled out from under me again? Yes, I think that part of my story may add an extra wrinkle to my situation in terms of where my psyche was at that point in time. Even though you know it's not personal, it still doesn't stop you from doubting yourself at least a little and questioning if it was based on *something* you did.

April 3, 2020 was my last day of work. I want to point out that I truly and optimistically assumed I'd be back at work by May, June at the latest. That the company would've already rebounded enough to bring back the eliminated positions too, including mine, and resume business as usual. But I soon found out this would not be the case.

During those earliest stages of quarantine, even when I was still working, I found myself—like so many others—thrust into a new environment but I tried to make the most of it. Part of me, a big part actually, was honestly relieved to some extent. I was somewhat naïve in terms of how long I thought this whole "thing" would last. News was flying in from so many different sources, from so many different "experts," and I didn't know what to believe, or what to think.

And, because I knew things were beyond my control, I took the approach of looking at the next few weeks (yes, I thought it would be "weeks") as a much-needed break and reprieve from the hustle and bustle of daily life: baseball practice, dance lessons, gymnastics, piano lessons, community events, school events, etc., etc. It was refreshing, and very much welcomed, to be able to take a step back and breathe, and almost relish the fact, that for the first time in recent memory, I didn't have a million places to be at one time. I could truly spend a night at home without feeling pressured or guilty, or having to worry about the next activity on the list, or ensuring my kids weren't even a half-second late to whatever event they were signed up for on that particular evening.

We transitioned to a life at home relatively seamlessly, enjoying activities like baking (yes, I baked—Mickey Mouse-shaped Beignets, thank you very much), experimenting with new recipes, playing games, building Legos (including a 4,000+ piece Disney Castle we used for a Fourth of July fireworks show that rivaled Disney World), watching movies, and just being at home to enjoy one another's company. I tapped into my creative side

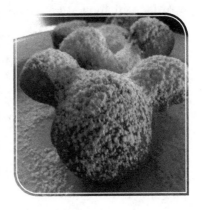

and learned how to create and edit videos, taught myself new skills and mastered new photo editing programs, and cherished the fact that, for once, I had nowhere to be. And, it seemed, we all were embracing this extra time  to be together and savored the downtime that was obviously missing as we rushed around, trying to keep up with the hectic pace of the daily grind. And that was pretty much how we spent the first six weeks of quarantine.

During this same time, with my wife, Kristie, still working (from home), and my three children adjusting to a new way of learning, I also assumed the positions of "homeschool dad" and CGCO—Chief Grilled Cheese Officer. I helped my three kids transition to their online learning curriculum. Due to the rapidly evolving situation, the school board essentially "flipped the switch" overnight and moved to an online learning environment, which, for the final few months of the school year, consisted primarily of online discussion boards and self-paced assignments with limited face-to-face interaction with, or instruction from, their teachers.

I am not complaining. The fact they were able to get the program and websites up and running as quickly as they did, while providing every student in the county with a loaner laptop as needed, was nothing short of miraculous. However, because most of the work was self-paced, my elementary-school-aged children (then a kindergartener, second grader, and fourth grader, respectively), needed more hands-on support. And, since I was not working, I found myself providing more of that than I would otherwise need to if they were in their normal classroom environment.

By May, we had adjusted to the "new normal" as well as I could have hoped, and, in fact, better than I expected. There were some hiccups along the way, like having to give the occasional reminder during tests that asking, "Hey, Alexa, what is 12 x 13?" wasn't exactly acceptable. Aside from that, all was fine and, shockingly, we were not that sick of each other's company, at least not that I was aware of anyway.

I will state, as there were no definitive signs indicating travel demand would pick up anytime soon, I was also in the process of looking and posting for other jobs. Often. Looking for a job became my job. My goal was to return to Marriott, but I realized the odds were probably pretty slim. Throughout this book, weaved in between birding trips and the lessons I learned, I'll tell stories about some of these interview experiences, and the jobs I felt very confident about, too.

So, yes, I will mention now, how a series of job rejections, one after another, also contributed to the emotional toll of the quarantine period and being out of work. A big toll, to be honest. It's one thing to have your position eliminated and career impacted by something beyond your control. But, when you finally have an opportunity to interview, and then experience the sting of rejection—several times in three of four months—that's different. Because then, even if it's still not about you personally, it sure feels like it is.

There were good moments and bad moments and they seemed to trade places with one another arbitrarily. I could be standing at the stove, making a grilled cheese sandwich for my kids, happy as could be, whistling away, and then a second later be overcome with sadness and grief for seemingly no reason. I could be watching a funny movie or show, laughing one moment and stone-faced the next without much warning—for myself or those around me.

I share all this to clarify, as much as I tried to focus on the positives that came with the extra family time, I still was looking for work the entire time. And, because I was, and failing at it, despite the optimistic disposition I tried to maintain, there were many moments when this was challenging to do. During those startling moments of darkness, I tried my best to avoid staying there for long. I wouldn't allow myself to. For one, it's because, as I have said before, I knew this wasn't about me. Plus, adding worry to an already unfortunate situation only exacerbates the issue and causes more unnecessary angst.

Nevertheless, during that early May timeframe, despite the ups and downs of my inner psyche, there were some positive signs the world itself was starting to open up again. Grocery stores began to resume normal hours. Restaurants, which had to rely solely on carryout and delivery service, began to reopen their dining rooms. And, most importantly and what became a central factor in my personal journey, county and state parks, which had been shuttered since March, were reopening as well. Dozens of places 15 minutes from me—with dozens more within 30 minutes or so—I never knew existed, would soon become my personal sanctuaries, even if I didn't know it just yet.

Everglades National Park was among them. Of course, I knew this park existed but had never been, despite living about an hour away. It was somewhere I'd wanted to visit since moving to Florida in 2013 but because of our jam-packed schedule, I hadn't carved out the time to make it happen. More on that in a moment.

Coincidentally, at this same time, my oldest son, Dylan, was assigned an end-of-year research project on, yes, you guessed it, Everglades National Park. As I was helping him, I found myself as engaged as he was in the assignment. We watched a documentary on National Geographic as part of his research.

Up to that point in my life, I had only experienced one National Park—Yellowstone. While growing up in the Washington, D.C., area, I was fortunate to visit other historic sites such as the Lincoln Memorial and the Washington Monument, and others within a couple hours' drive, in places like Philadelphia, home of the Liberty Bell, but I was fairly sheltered as it related to my own exposure to some of the most majestic and magnificent places our country had to offer.

Visiting Yellowstone, however, left quite an indelible mark on me. Back in 2003, before Kristie and I were married, to celebrate my college graduation and her completion of graduate school, we visited her father (now my father-in-law) for a week when he was living in Bozeman, Montana. It remains one of the most enjoyable and memorable vacations of my life, and our three daytrips to Yellowstone National Park were certainly a contributing factor.

Perhaps because of my own family's hustle-and-bustle lifestyle growing up, with youth sports seemingly dictating our calendar, I had never experienced such a place, and before my first visit when I was 23, I didn't know the difference between Yellowstone and Jellystone. I knew Yogi and Boo-Boo lived at one, but it would have been a coin flip to determine which. Between the waterfalls and geysers (Old Faithful), the wildlife (notably bears and, no, not Yogi) and the historical significance as our country's first National Park, I was fascinated.

When learning about the Everglades, as popular as Yellowstone in its own right, and essentially in my "backyard," I fondly recalled that trip taken 17 years earlier and watched the documentary with extreme curiosity. What stood out, as one might assume, was hearing about the more than 350 species of birds that live there throughout the year. If you thought I was going to say alligators, need I remind you that you're reading a book with birds in the title?

Incidentally, the documentary included a feature on Great egrets, which, as I'll share in a future chapter, are fascinating in many ways. I've loved to photograph them but, if this doesn't remind you that wildlife includes the term "wild" for a reason, then I am not sure what will. When egrets are born, the siblings will fight one another for food and in some cases, the stronger ones will sense weakness in his siblings and kill them to ensure he gets more food. As I watched this video, almost in disbelief, with the mom egret looking as if everything was just fine, with an, "Oh, nothing to see here," expression on her face, I said to Dylan, "I guess I shouldn't give you as much grief as I do for picking on your brother. At least you haven't tried to kill him for more food. Yet."

After all this, I was more motivated than ever to experience the Everglades in person, which brings me back to the above point about the parks. Within days of this assignment, the

Everglades, like most of the National Parks, started a phased reopening. As an added perk, the standard $20 daily admission fee was waved, since many of the park's attractions were still closed. The free admission days were part of the country's effort to encourage people to explore its many great places while practicing safe social distancing at the same time.

Since school was still self-paced, I told the kids if they got their work done early that day, we could go on a little field trip. While I stated before that they didn't always respond to our summer field trips with what you'd call enthusiasm, at that point they hadn't really left the house in two months, so they were jumping at the chance to get out. The fact they got to "leave school early" in their minds (which just meant they finished their required assignments ahead of schedule), was a bonus.

Around mid-morning on Thursday May 7, 2020, we packed some snacks, sunscreen, and of course, the most important accompaniment for a trip to the Everglades at the onset of summer, bug-spray, and we ventured out, ready to see some action. We saw… nothing. Not a single creature as far as the eye could see. Except an incredibly bright yellow grasshopper which I

later learned was an Eastern Lubber Grasshopper and a favorite among Everglades' visitors. Still, not exactly enough to compel someone to visit the park for the first time. But it did not matter. While we didn't see anything else interesting in terms of wildlife, we had an entire National Park to ourselves. For free. How often will you get that opportunity in life? Not very often.

Similar to my experience at Yellowstone, my day at the Everglades with Dylan, Emma, and Noah, was special. Again, not because of what we saw, which wasn't much. But it was the middle of the day in the middle of the week. I wasn't checking email. I wasn't worried about driving back to get them to practice. I was simply living in the moment and taking it in. It was the beginning of what would soon become my "therapy" for the next few months, even if I didn't realize it at the time.

When we got home, I decided to see if there were other places closer that could provide similar experiences but within minutes and for free (indefinitely not just temporarily) and searched online for "Best birding sites in Broward County." I was pleasantly surprised to find several them so close but was quite shocked to discover the top-rated spot in the area, by many accounts, was a place three miles from me and, ironically, somewhere I'd been close to a dozen times. Plantation Preserve Linear Trail, connected to the golf club of the same name, Plantation Preserve. Even my kids have taken lessons and attended summer camp there. And yet, somehow, I never knew there was a nature trail running along the north side of the driving range where I whacked away at little white balls for years.

If that doesn't help to illustrate how easy it is to get caught up in our own routines without taking the time to enjoy what is right at our fingertips, I don't know what does. Here I was, just a few feet away from one of South Florida's most popular destinations for nature enthusiasts and bird lovers alike, and yet I had no idea it was even there. And this would be the case for dozens of other parks throughout Broward County as well as our neighbors to the north and south, Palm Beach and Miami-Dade Counties, respectively.

I went to bed that night excited, and since I was finally coming to grips with knowing I most likely would not be going back to work anytime soon, decided to declare summer 2020 the summer of Florida exploration.

Things were being set in motion, with several driving forces converging at once to create a "perfect storm" of sorts, explaining how and why I got into birding when I did. The Everglades project and subsequent trip, the discovery of parks closer to me that offered incredible opportunities for exploring nature, and the fact that I would still be out of work and transitioning from "homeschool dad" to "camp counselor dad." Also, the startling revelation that all of this had been so close to me for nearly seven years, and I squandered countless opportunities to take advantage of it because there was always something else "more important" to do. For the first time in my adult life, that would no longer be the case.

The final factor that became the tipping point happened just three days after my visit to the Everglades. It was Mother's Day, May 10, and my mom, Ruth, and stepdad, Rick, came over for dinner. It was the first time we had seen them since March 7, at Dylan's first (and sadly last) little league baseball game of the year. We dined on the patio because there was still some wariness about being indoors together, and we were able to enjoy one another's company on a relatively mild May evening while sharing our own personal observations and experiences of life under quarantine.

I had told my mom the story about the Everglades and my recent discovery of the Plantation Preserve Linear Trail. She and Rick were also frequent visitors of the adjacent golf club—much more frequent than me—and she, too, had no idea this trail existed.

"You want to check it out this week?" I asked. "We can go at 7 a.m. one day so I can still be home in time to get the kids set up for the school day."

"Sure, I'd love to!" my mom replied.

It was settled. The following Thursday, May 14, we were going to meet at the Linear Trail and dip our toes into the world of birding.

Now, even though you are already aware that birding changed my perspective and outlook on life over the last few months—and to some degree my life itself—when we agreed to meet that morning, none of that was on my mind. How could it have been? Other than embarking on some sort of religious or spiritual pilgrimage or joining something like the Peace Corps, for example, I can't imagine there are many activities you enter knowing they will have such a profound impact on you before you even try them for the first time.

I could be wrong, but the first time Billy Joel sat down at the piano, it's safe to assume he wasn't inspired to become the Piano Man *before* his fingers "tickled the ivories" for the first time, even if his father was a classical pianist (which he was). I'll cut Billy some slack, though, considering he was four years old when he began playing, and was probably more interested in knowing when nap time was.

What makes the point even more is that about three weeks before this, as I was continuing to look for fun stay-at-home activities for the kids and I to enjoy, my mom asked me one evening if I thought we would enjoy a bird feeder. I immediately squashed the idea. "Sounds like a headache. Any other ideas?"

Honestly, I laugh because as I write this, I have three feeders, each with a unique type of seed, and a bird bath. What can I say? This is what it looks like when a hobby becomes a passion. Which leads me to another point I should mention. I am a person with varied and numerous interests, so many people gave me a hard time (jokingly, for the most part) when I first started showing an interest in birding and dismissed it as my "flavor of the week."

I am—how one personality test described me—an enthusiast. I don't always put a ton of stock into those sorts of things but that one pretty much nailed it. Enthusiasts find pleasure in seeking new experiences, exploring new interests, and immersing themselves in different activities that bring joy and fulfill their desire to discover new activities that enable them to take advantage of everything life has to offer. It's highly doubtful the late culinary rebel, Anthony Bourdain, took this same test (or any personality test) but I always remembered the biography portion of his Twitter profile simply stated: Enthusiast. If that's the company I keep, I'll take it.

Sometimes these interests and new activities turn into passions and sometimes they don't, and this is a point I dive into in chapter 4. Sometimes they are simply things that piqued my curiosity at one point in time but as far back as I can remember, I have taken an interest in a number of different things that seem to have a randomness to them. As in, how could someone who is crazy about sports be equally crazy about music, and not just music, but everything from The Beatles to Garth Brooks, Frank Sinatra to Taylor Swift, Guns N' Roses to Billy Joel, and everything in between? How could someone approach attending a live sporting event with the same enthusiasm and excitement as going to history museums, art exhibits, rock concerts, Broadway musicals, theme parks, wine shops, or even bookstores? I don't know. But I am okay with it. Eclectic, eccentric, diverse. These are all words I've heard to describe my—I guess you could say—zest for life.

Some of these other passions will be referenced in this book to either help reinforce a particular lesson or help add context to one I learned on the birding trail. I did that intentionally because it gives you greater insight into the person who wrote the words you are reading. And, perhaps, that makes the stories you'll read in the coming pages and the lessons that follow in the subsequent chapters resonate a little more than they would have.

In any case, birdwatching, I thought, would be another activity to add to my wide variety of interests, even if casually and enjoyed every now and again. The point is, it's important to keep in mind I arrived that morning and looked at it the same way I would if someone invited me to go shoot pool or play poker.

They say that certain people come into your life "for a

reason, a season, or a lifetime." Well, maybe certain hobbies do, too. And I'd like to make an edit to this popular saying if I may. I think it should be, "for a lifetime or a season but *always* for a reason," because maybe sometimes we do find a specific hobby that fills a need for a specific period of time—for a season. Even if we no longer find ourselves doing it or needing to do it, it doesn't mean that this particular hobby wasn't meaningful and needed at that point in our lives.

So, if I went to Plantation Preserve once and that was it, that's fine. If nothing else, it was a chance to get out of the house and enjoy some fresh air with my mom as we visited a new park for the first time. Not a bad Thursday morning if that was all it turned out to be.

The day we were supposed to meet at the Preserve had arrived and I pulled into the parking lot without expectations that it would be anything spectacular. As in, I wasn't prepared to have "my mind blown" or anything. Certainly, I didn't realize

how it would, in hindsight, be one of the defining moments of the year, if not my life. After all, not even a month earlier I adamantly rejected my mother's gracious offer to buy me a bird feeder.

We met at the trail entrance—with our masks on, of course—and set out on our first expedition. I'll pause here and say, if you're reading this in 2031 and not 2021 and somehow forgot these were a "thing," yes, they were. Also, I am glad this photo exists for two reasons. One, it serves as a symbol of the beginning of my birding journey and two, that "Speaking Words of Wisdom" Beatles mask was my favorite (I figured if I was going to wear one, might as well wear one that captured my personality), but I lost it at some point that summer and was never able to find another one. But it lives on forever with this lone picture.

Within minutes, I was hooked. My first observation was a Limpkin (at the time, I had no idea what a Limpkin was, let alone that I had just seen one). But it didn't matter. I started snapping away. I got some amazing shots. And that

A Limpkin with a morning snack. May 2020, Plantation, Fla.

was just the start. Before the morning walk ended, I saw a Tri-Colored Heron, Green Heron, Great Egret, White Ibis, and several other species, each more fascinating than the next.

Of course, when I saw all those different birds that morning, I had no clue that's what they were—just like with the

Limpkin. This wasn't a roadblock but a springboard. I wanted to know. I wanted to learn more.

When I got home, I uploaded my pictures and was hooked all over again. Because as fun as it is to see and observe an interesting new bird, I soon learned it's equally fun, if not more, to comb through the photos to identify exactly what you saw (or thought you saw) and photographed. Here is the thing, and perhaps the best part of this entire journey, and why I felt the need to give the additional context of my inclination to try new hobbies and explore new interests. Because when I showed up on May 14, it was still just a birding trip. That is, everything I talked about in the preface—the self-reflection, the discovery, the journey to find happiness, and the countless lessons that now fill the pages of this book—this was not even a blip on my radar screen, even if I found the morning's outing to be extremely enjoyable.

I had no idea what started out as a research project on the Everglades would lead to something that would be the single biggest factor in my ability to move forward in a positive way as I continued to cope with being unemployed and dealt with several job rejections that would come in the months ahead that left me wondering if I'd ever work again. If I'd ever feel normal again, and, honestly, without the birds, I don't know how I would have.

There is a country song by the popular artist Trace Atkins called *Just Fishin'* that tells the story of a series of father-daughter fishing trips that were more than just fishing trips. Even if the young girl in the song was unaware, her father knew they were about something much bigger: the memories they were making and the experiences they were enjoying together.

In that same vein, at that point, I thought I was "just birding." But all of that was about to change. I was about to find out what the little birdies were going to tell me, and it was all thanks to a bright red Northern Cardinal.

Chapter 1

POSITIVITY: THE NORTHERN CARDINAL

"If you ever doubt the universe is conspiring good things for you, remember your Cardinal."

— *My Mother, Ruth*

The Northern Cardinal, taken May 21, 2020, at the Plantation Preserve Linear Trail, Plantation, Florida.

My first time going to the Plantation Preserve Linear Trail to look for birds with my mother was nothing more than what it sounded like. We were there that Thursday morning, May 14, 2020, as we had discussed doing on Mother's Day five days earlier, simply to see what interesting bird species we'd be able to observe at this veritable sanctuary that neither of us knew existed a week before that initial visit. I didn't know if I would enjoy the experience enough to want to do it a second time; I was just there to try something new.

Regardless of what would end up happening, we were both equally excited to be there. For one, this was only the second time we had seen each other since March, despite living less than five miles apart. And two, we were both, I think, suffering from a little bit of cabin fever. As much as I was enjoying the downtime at home—and I was—I am an extrovert at heart and someone who basically craves social interaction and experiencing new things. And I am, after all, my mother's son, thus I had an inkling she was going a tad stir crazy, too.

Other than the periodic trips to Publix (and the one trip to the Everglades), I hadn't really been out of the house since March 13—the final day my children were actually *in* school, officially signaling the onset of quarantine. This also meant that I hadn't put on a pair of pants in two months, something that—to this day—I am quite proud of, in fact. I chuckle as I share the following story.

One night around that time, I made the following statement during dinner.

"When this whole thing is over, I'm going to invest in some new mesh gym shorts. I have worn nothing but mesh shorts for two months. I am just rotating the same three pairs and doing laundry every two to three days. The people at Publix are going to think I own only one outfit."

"Dad, I know," my then-five-year-old Emma said with such an endearing innocence, and her voice filled with enough enthusiasm to make your heart burst. "Here's what you can do! You can pretend you didn't lose your job, and you can wear your jeans or regular pants to the store, and then just tell them you're on your way home from work or something."

I laughed so hard and alas, I needed to do a load of laundry more quickly than I anticipated.

I felt the need to share that additional context because sometimes we don't choose which hobbies will turn into passions. Sometimes, they choose us. And I also now believe sometimes they choose *when* to find us. And this was the day I began to realize that maybe there was something more at play.

Back to the Preserve. One week after our initial visit, on Thursday, May 21, 2020, I met my mother around the same time I did the Thursday before but with one minor difference. My mother, always the early riser, beat me by about 15 minutes.

This isn't newsworthy, considering she has been getting up at 5:30 a.m. forever, and still does even though she is retired. I, on the other hand, had to peel myself out of bed at 6:45 to give myself a fighting chance to be there by the 7:00 time we agreed to meet that day. I got up, looked at my phone to see 6:50 and fired off a quick, "I'm on my way," text which was code for, "I just got up, so I need to brush my teeth, do some other 'morning business,' throw on some clothes, then make some coffee, drink some coffee, check Facebook, and putter around for an extra five minutes for no real reason, then I'll be on my way."

On that second morning, I was the *early bird that got the worm*. While this isn't newsworthy either, it's noteworthy because it can be seen as early indication that this was not only where I wanted to be but needed to be. I found myself there by 6:45 when we agreed to meet at 7:00, when the previous week I hadn't been awake at that time of morning yet. As I waited for my mom, I enjoyed seeing the sun rise over the golf course, which was also starting to reopen as it, too, had been closed since mid-March. It was nice to see as I took it as another sign things were slowly returning to normal.

My mom arrived and we began to walk the trail as the sounds of metal clubs hitting golf balls echoed in the distance, and, of course, as the sounds of birds chirping filled the air. While this was the second time my mother and I walked the

Preserve Trail together, it was my fourth time. I almost felt guilty when I casually mentioned it that morning, but I had managed to sneak over there twice the previous weekend, but only for about 10 minutes or so each time as I was on the way to, yes, Publix. If you're wondering why I felt guilty, I suppose it's because maybe I saw it as "our" thing and not "my" thing. Not yet anyway.

My mom of course was fine with it, and it's funny to think about now but looking back, I am glad I had that talk with her. It almost gave me the permission, in a sense, to start seeking out new adventures solo without hurting my mom's feelings or making her feel left out. Besides, we would continue our walks, regardless of how often I ventured out on my own expeditions. Still, it was somewhat of a relief to get that off my chest and, also, I knew our weekly walks would continue. And they do.

As my mom and I wandered through the Preserve, I said to her, "I really want to find a bright red bird. I don't even know why. But I want to get a photo of a Cardinal or something."

This was before I had read any books about birds, (I ordered one later that day), and, also, long before my days of using eBird.com, the site to track observations and seek out potential sites where specific birds have most recently been seen. This to emphasize the point that my random desire to see a Cardinal that day was just that, random. Not only random but I didn't even know if it was a realistic desire either, as my knowledge of the common species in Florida was still fairly limited at this point. Meaning non-existent.

You'll read stories later when I went to a specific park looking for a specific bird. But not this day. I could easily have had the same desire to see a penguin, and, if so, I would *not* have been able to see one, regardless of my desire to do so. Extreme example, but in my earliest days of birding, not a far-fetched thing for me to have thought, to be honest. Do we have penguins in Fort Lauderdale?

So, I said it without knowing if it was within the realm of possibility. And no offense to my mom, she probably didn't know either. The other thing I would be remiss if I didn't mention here is while I said in the preface that this journey was about the lessons I learned on my own last summer, it goes far beyond that.

This lesson that I am about to share now was 100 percent influenced by my mom. At the risk of sounding too philosophical, and, perhaps, even cheesy, it's almost as if my mom helping provide this one key lesson for me that day at the earliest stages of my journey, was the turning point and is what then allowed me to *leave the nest* (see, I told you it was cheesy, but certainly fitting). I needed the guidance that sometimes only a parent or parental figure could give before I sought out the other lessons that fill the remaining pages of this book. Because true growth, learning, and healing would have to come through my own sense of discovery, not through someone else's.

After I shared my desire to see a Cardinal, my mom, ever positive, would say things such as, "Well, just keep saying it out loud and thinking it and the universe will bring it to you." To be honest, my reactions to these statements from my dear mother are usually a combination of, "Okay Mom" mixed with a slight eye roll. It's not that I didn't think positive thinking was a good way to go through life, I was just slightly more cynical, I guess. Especially at that time, as much as I probably didn't want to admit it. My mom is the most positive person I've ever known. She has been giving me that kind of advice for years, and it wasn't because she was simply a mother trying to reassure her son that all would be well. It is just *who* she is and how everyone knows her.

It doesn't come as naturally to me. While I do think of myself as a glass-half-full person, I also know that my glass is still half full. It is never overflowing. My mom, on the other hand, doesn't have enough glasses to contain her positivity. As we continued our walk, we saw dozens of birds, but, alas, nothing red as far as the eye could see. I wasn't too upset about it though. As I shared, there would be plenty of outings when I went out in search of a specific bird and then ran the risk of leaving disappointed if I didn't. This time, it was an "Oh well, next time" kind of feeling as I headed home.

Here is where the true lesson comes into play. I uploaded my photos to my computer when I got home and started to click through. I only took about 15, and as I clicked to the last photo of the day, there he was: a bright red Northern Cardinal perched on a high branch about 50-60 feet away from me. You may be curious how I didn't know I took that photo. Simple. One, it was off in the distance a bit and I couldn't tell what it was, and two, sometimes the perspective at which we are coming from makes the color of a bird hard to determine (more on that in later chapters). But I definitely noticed *something* up there that compelled me to snap away.

I texted my mom right away and asked, "Mom, what would you call this?" along with the photo of the Cardinal I had unknowingly photographed not even an hour earlier.

My mom replied, "I call it *exactly* what we were talking about. You thought about it and brought it to you," followed by just a few heart emojis for good measure. My mom is always good for a few of those...a few too many if you ask me but like I said, it's part of her good-natured spirit. She followed that up with, "If you ever doubt the universe is conspiring good things for you, remember your Cardinal."

I sat there for a second, smiling and somewhat bewildered. Could there be more to this whole concept of "thinking positive thoughts and trusting the universe to take care of the rest" than

I was willing to admit? Let it be said, this is not necessarily an original concept and as much as I admire my mother's wisdom, I am not crediting her for developing this philosophy either. In fact, there are many books on this subject that discuss this concept of the power of positive thinking, including one with that exact title. *The Power of Positive Thinking* was published in 1952, and not to give my mom's age away, I'll just say this was at least three years before she was even born. I kind of gave it away, didn't I, with the specificity of three years? Sorry, mom.

The Secret, which discusses how positive thoughts and the laws of attraction co-exist, is another one. And there are a million books out there that focus on this, so I don't want to usurp their spotlight too much, because my book is not meant to be in the same category as any of those. However, the one my mother was telling me about earlier that morning is called *E-Squared* by Pam Grout, which as the description on Amazon states, "could best be described as a lab manual with simple experiments to prove once and for all that reality is malleable, that consciousness trumps matter, and that you shape your life with your mind...to prove there really is a positive, loving, totally hip force in the universe."

This is a weighty concept but also fascinating to think about—that maybe, just maybe, we have more control over these sorts of things than we realize we do. I am not an expert on this and haven't done the research that these other authors have done, so I am not claiming to own this philosophy as my own. In fact, I don't even know how all this works.

I am not suggesting this is like *Aladdin* where you rub a lamp, a genie pops out, and your wish comes true. I don't think any of these authors are suggesting this either, by the way. I may even be oversimplifying it so, if you're saying to yourself, "Gee, Matt, if only it were so easy. Just put it out there and make it happen"—I get it. Trust me. But, if you allow yourself to contemplate it for a moment, why not think that way? Because as I shared a couple paragraphs above, while I have never described myself as a bastion of positivity, I have always believed in looking at things with an optimistic lens and in seeing challenges as opportunities. If for no other reason than it certainly doesn't hurt to look at life that way.

I want to be cognizant about reading too much into something every time I encounter a teeny bit of good luck. For example, if I were to enter a seemingly full parking lot and a front-row spot becomes available as soon as I pull in, I'm not going to automatically presume there was something cosmic at play, and that the universe gave me a front-row parking spot while making somebody else walk the 1,000 feet in the pouring rain to the entrance.

It could be easy to look at everything as a "sign" that, "yep, there's that universe again taking good care of me." It isn't necessarily a bad thing to think this; however, the reason why I say this, is because you also can't (or shouldn't) assume the opposite to be true either. As in, looking at it as a "sign" that the universe is conspiring *against* you, just because you don't find that front-row parking spot, and you are the one that's then forced to walk the 1,000 feet in the rain. If you put all your stock into this concept, then I think that, yes, you can run the risk of driving yourself crazy, trying to determine what is simply a case of good (or bad) luck versus the universe helping you when you need it.

As I see it, I think both things can be true. They can co-exist. Sometimes it is simply luck, and sometimes there is more to it and it's not entirely up to us to decipher between the two. I am reminded of that funny, yet lesser known, John Travolta film, *Michael*, where he plays an angel, co-starring William Hurt and Andie McDowell.

The three of them are joking one morning as Michael, the angel played by Travolta, tries to explain how angels work and they aren't always capable of pulling off huge miracles, rather sometimes small ones. He then mentioned that some angels waste their powers on seemingly trivial things and in "stupid ways," though he didn't want to be specific. William Hurt, who plays a skeptical journalist on assignment with Michael then asks, "you mean like the parking space angels?"

"I don't like to criticize other angels," Michael quips back.

Whether or not there are parking space angels, or the universe helped you find a parking space, I want to emphasize that I think it's important to think positive thoughts, but it is equally important to not become cynical and overly skeptical when those positive thoughts do not yield the results you hoped for, and you make your way to the entrance from the last row of the parking lot in the middle of a downpour.

By the way, the universe, I don't believe, ever conspires against us. That sort of mentality is what leads to these "woe is me" thoughts I have tried my best to avoid (even though losing my job gave me a few of these). I think it's more that we aren't always aware of what the ultimate plan is. Even if, at the time, it might feel that the world is, for some reason, out to get us.

While seeing a Cardinal was not exactly a rare sighting, truth be told, I had no clue if it was when I said it and that is significant. Because what started as a random and possibly unrealistic desire about seeing a Cardinal turned into the central lesson—on positivity—that would guide and govern my actions for the remainder of the summer, and, with any hope, the rest of my life.

With this lesson, there is another hidden within it. As hidden perhaps as a Cardinal in a far-away tree. What I was looking for was right in front of me and I didn't even know it.

Sometimes, what we seek is right there, right within our grasp. It's up to us to pay attention and notice it and take advantage of the opportunity to seize it.

I spent the rest of the day still somewhat baffled by the entire thing, in a good way, of course. It compelled me to write my first LinkedIn blog since the pandemic started. As a final takeaway, I left this piece of parting advice to close: "Whether or not you are among those who have been facing uncertainties or feeling as though your world has been turned upside down, just remember to take a breath, look up, and go find that Red Cardinal."

The feedback was positive, which was nice, but more importantly, it seemed that the message itself resonated with others. As if I somehow was able to articulate certain things people were feeling too but couldn't articulate or didn't feel comfortable doing so publicly. So, that day, May 21, 2020, was not only the turning point in my journey because of the experience with the Cardinal but because of my decision to write about it and share insights as I found myself looking for my own positive signs.

I continued to write all summer. The more I wrote, the more vulnerable and open I became. People responded to it. Allowing myself to be honest and real without the need to stand behind a "Oh, everything's just fine" façade enabled me to find the peace and growth I was seeking. If I wasn't willing to do that, then finding inner peace and growth would be like looking for a penguin in Fort Lauderdale.

As I close this chapter, here is an additional tidbit to ponder. The bird I saw more than any other all summer, no matter where I was: The Northern Cardinal. Including Tallahassee during a road trip to see my brother and his family, which continued into Delaware to see my dad and stepmom, Wendy, where the same thing was true. My family and I went to Hilton Head, South Carolina, in the middle of August for one final getaway before school started (a trip that was already mostly paid for a year ago) and the first bird I saw when I stepped out on to the balcony after we arrived, was, once again, a Northern Cardinal.

And the more I saw him, the more vivid he became, and the more often he appeared, the closer and more visible he would be. I have some photos that appear as though we are standing next to each other, chatting about life. The photo on the cover of this book is one such example. And even though I saw dozens of Cardinals over the next few months, in my mind and in my heart, it was always the same one. That first one I saw on May 21, the day it really all began. With my mom, from a distance when I needed to and didn't even realize just how much I did.

One final note. I alluded to this already when I said it was the last photo that I took that day. It's because I saw the

Cardinal on the way out as we were exiting the trail, heading back to our cars. And when I stopped, my mom didn't see it—only I did. When I said I saw something but wasn't sure what, I did at least notice something compelling. My mom didn't see it at all. This is not a knock on her vision, because she's pointed out plenty of birds to me that she saw first. Maybe it's because he appeared for me, as a sign for me and not necessarily for anyone else, not even my own mom.

You see, the Cardinal, the one who seemed to show up that day only for me when I didn't even know it, remained with me all summer to serve as a reminder, as my mom said, that the universe was indeed conspiring good things for me. And the lesson on positivity would be the basis for all the subsequent lessons that now follow. Without the "stay positive and think optimistically" concept top of mind throughout the rest of my endeavors, I likely would not have experienced the same types of revelations that summer.

This was the day I finally started to get that there was something bigger than me and my situation in play. But the journey was just beginning.

A LITTLE BIRDIE TOLD ME...

Chapter 2

PROGRESSION: THE EGRET AND THE OVENBIRD (NO, NOT TURKEYS)

"Dad, I can't do this!"— My Daughter, Emma
"Yes, you can. And if you can't, you'll learn how."— Me

The Great Egret taken May 2020, Kendall, Florida

There are certain sayings or expressions that have entered our country's collective lexicon at one point or another and have somehow become part of the fabric of our society. They are designed to help people, usually children, visualize the words to make it easier to get the core meaning of a lesson.

"Don't judge a book by its cover," makes getting the point across to a child a little easier when trying to explain why it's important to not make false assumptions about a person based on their physical appearance. The child can picture a book in their head, maybe one that looked boring or dull from the outside, but a book they really enjoyed once they gave it a chance.

There are also, oddly enough, several that come to mind from the birding world. "Don't count your chickens before they hatch," "Don't put all your eggs in one basket," and "A bird in the hand is worth two in the bush," are all popular sayings we use every day to help teach lifelong lessons to our kids on a given topic. If one of my kids is celebrating prematurely about how they're about to win whatever video game they're playing, I'll say "Now, now, don't count your chickens before they hatch."

By the way, if you thought I was going to say, "Kill two birds with one stone," when I started rattling off examples of bird-inspired idioms, then all I have to say is shame on you.

While we use these to teach lessons to our children, and

we ourselves have been hearing them forever, as adults, we aren't always great about keeping these lessons top of mind. And, sometimes, they only occur to us in hindsight. This is the case for me as I began to dive into birding head-first following my first few visits to the Plantation Preserve. Not necessarily realizing it at the time, I was learning, or being reminded of, the age-old lesson that "You have to learn to crawl before you can walk."

Like the adages above, crawling before you walk is sage advice that we give to anyone starting a new hobby. It's a great way to reinforce the need to take "baby steps" as they approach a new endeavor. Otherwise, they run the risk of potentially becoming easily discouraged if they don't find immediate success. In this chapter, I'll introduce a new one: "Egrets before Ovenbirds." And I'll explain why shortly.

My son, Noah, the musician of the family, has been playing piano for a little over two years. For my fortieth birthday, I told his teacher I wanted him to learn my favorite Billy Joel song, *And So it Goes*. It is a fairly complicated piece but compared to some of his other compositions, it is one of his more approachable songs. Even still, I knew it would be a challenge for Noah, but I wanted him to have the challenge because it would push him to become a better piano player in the end.

That's somewhat of a separate lesson though. How it fits into this chapter is based on the following additional context.

I only made the request after Noah had been playing piano for about 18 months, and after he received high marks from a third-party judge during his Piano Guild audition in July 2019. (My fortieth birthday wasn't until June 2020, so I also gave him ample time, too, but that's also somewhat beside the point). Here is the point: I made the request after Noah had already tasted early success in the hobby, and *after* I knew he was capable of pulling it off, even if I knew it would still be a challenge.

If Noah were a first-year piano player or, worse yet, someone who never played before, then there is no way I would have made such a daunting request. It would be unfair and almost cruel of me. Imagine a novice who never touched a piano before, then feeling the pressure to learn a song that was composed by one of the most popular modern-day rock musicians of all-time? He'd have made one attempt and likely never want to see a piano, let alone play one, ever again.

No, I only made the request *after* Noah had spent 18 months learning to crawl before he could walk. But as is the case with teaching many of these lessons to our kids, we don't always heed our own advice. Maybe because we are adults and think we've learned it all already. At this point in our lives, we don't need such basic life lessons instilled in us because, presumably, we've achieved a fair amount of success in our own lives thus far and so we feel as though we have it covered. Again, this is a mistake.

Thankfully, this is a lesson I did not have to learn the hard way. Perhaps, like my Northern Cardinal appearing without me realizing I needed to see him, the birds knew this was a lesson they needed to teach me without me necessarily realizing it as well. Then again, it could be a great coincidence, but here is the lesson.

I shared already that I discovered birding as a hobby, thanks to a few factors that came to a head around the same time in mid-May. At that point, I couldn't begin to guess which birds were only here periodically as visitors or "migrants" and which live here year-round as "residents." When I finally received my first book, the *Birds of Florida,* I became somewhat dismayed to discover, not only had I *just* missed spring migration right before I started birding, but the birds I missed seeing by about a week or two, were some of the most colorful and marvelous that call Florida home, for part of the year anyway.

It was almost cruel in a way to think, had I just begun this a little earlier, I'd have had the opportunity to observe dozens and dozens more species, and not only that but the spectacular looking, too—the Painted Bunting being a prime example. This colorful bird graces the cover of a different Florida birds book that both my mom and my nephew, Johnny, happen to own. And he is a well-deserving cover model. With his red, blue, yellow, and green plumage, the Painted Bunting is also sometimes referred to as the rainbow bird and is arguably one of the most sought-after species in terms of photography among avid birders and casual observers alike. But, alas, as I would find out the day that I began to browse through the book I bought on May 21, they are only found in my neck of the woods in South Florida from October (September in rare instances) through April.

How unfortunate? What are the odds? What bad luck? Phooey!

Okay, I haven't said "phooey" since, well, never. But I was a tad disappointed at the thought I just missed the opportunity to see some of these birds and I'd have to wait four or five months before that opportunity came back again. However, I was unknowingly learning how to crawl before I walked. I spent the first few months then focusing on observing species that were here year-round, because frankly I had no other choice. But the reason why this was a lesson I was unaware of at the time, is because many of the birds I was observing are easier to observe. Not only due to the fact they are here all year long thus giving you more opportunities to see them, but also because a lot of them were larger, wading birds that don't provide much of a challenge at all to not only see them, but see them up close and photograph them.

I was able to "cut my teeth," to borrow another cliché, by looking for and photographing birds such as egrets (notably

Great, Cattle, and Snowy), Herons (Little Blue, Great Blue, Tricolored Heron, Green), Wood Storks, Anhingas, Limpkins, as well as several others like them. These birds are not only large, they tend to not move very fast either nor very often. They are extraordinarily patient as they sit by the water and look for their next meal—fish, of course.

One day last summer, while my kids and I were fishing, right alongside us, no more than five feet away, was a heron. He stayed there the whole time; despite the fact we were competing for the same fish. And maybe that's why he stayed. We'd lure the fish over with our bait, catch and release, and there the Heron would be waiting to snatch an unsuspecting fish who was just about to breathe a sigh of relief after his "near death experience" seconds earlier before I unhooked him and set him free. Either way, the Heron did not move the entire time.

Heron, August 2020, Plantation, Fla.

I brought up fishing here intentionally because it serves as a great reinforcement of this concept. When I moved to Florida in November 2013, one of my first purchases was a fishing rod. With lakes, ponds, and canals seemingly on every other corner like a Starbucks would be in New York City, there is no shortage of opportunities to go fishing year-round in South Florida and you'd never have to go very far to find a great spot. We went once during our first fall here and even though Dylan and Noah were young, they loved it (Emma was not

Fishing Trips: 2013 (above) and 2020 (below). Plantation, Fla.

born yet). They talked about it all the time and asked when we would be able to go again. I would always say something like, "Yes, soon. We just need to find a free weekend to do it."

That "free weekend," meaning the second fishing excursion we enjoyed in South Florida since moving here, was…last summer on the day we hung out with the Heron. Seriously. The reason I shared this experience is because it is the perfect example of allowing yourself the chance to crawl before you walk. Or, more specifically, what happens when you do not allow yourself to.

My family and I didn't spend much time exploring the great outdoors growing up. Not that we didn't make time for fun family adventures, we did, it's just that fishing, hiking, and visiting National

Parks were not part of the mix. We spent many weekends attending professional sporting events and, my older brother John and I, played sports year-round as well. My father even coached my little league baseball and youth footballs teams, too, throughout my childhood.

Those days spent at Dogwood Park in Rockville, Maryland, are undoubtedly among the greatest memories of my childhood. My dad and I, to this day, still talk about our dramatic come-from-behind win in the RBBA pee-wee division championship game in 1991. And, now that I am a father, who has served as an assistant on several of Dylan's and Noah's teams over the years, I have a greater appreciation than ever for my dad volunteering his time to be my coach for so many years.

I had a great childhood and was fortunate in so many ways. It's simply that fishing, among other outdoor hobbies, was not part of our family's collection of activities. As a result, that first time I took the boys fishing in 2013, it was actually *my* first time fishing too. Yes, I went fishing for the first time when I was 33 years old. And I had no idea what I was doing, got frustrated when the bait kept falling off the hook, even more frustrated when the line became tangled, and yet even more when I couldn't figure out how to reline it. Time to call it. We headed home that November morning disgruntled. I should say I did. My boys, then just four and two, respectively, didn't care. They were just happy to be out there with me. Yet another lesson I wouldn't understand until this past summer either.

So, when my sons continued to ask me over the next six years, when we could go fishing again, naturally I was reluctant to do so based on the failure of that first time. I didn't have the confidence to think I'd be able to find success trying a second time nor did I think I was capable of teaching my sons how to fish. And how could I when I didn't know either? Instead, I gave up and made excuses for why we hadn't been able to find the time again when, in actuality, it's because I was afraid of failing again. If you're asking what made me change my mind this past summer, I wish I could say that I had grown enough to not care whether I succeeded or not. But, no, not at that point anyway.

I mentioned in the last chapter a road trip last summer to see family that included a stop in Tallahassee where my brother, John, his wife, Billie, and their five kids live. Johnny, who is two months older than Dylan, was the one who taught my kids and me how to fish. Read that again.

Johnny and Dylan. July 2020. Tallahassee, Fla.

My 10-year-old nephew taught me how to fish. My sister-in-law, Billie, incidentally, *does* come from a family that spent more time engaging in activities like that and her uncle is an avid fisherman, thus Johnny learned from him too. Certainly, my brother was not the one to teach him.

Not only did I not have the confidence to want to try fishing again (or attempt to teach my sons how to again), I didn't want to admit that to the friends I had met down here since moving to Florida. Friends who grew up fishing and would have been more than happy to show me the ropes.

Yet more lessons. One, don't be embarrassed when you don't know something, and, therefore, don't be afraid to ask questions. This was a lesson I continued to learn through my birding endeavors, and there is a chapter on this later. So, I'll give myself some credit because when it came to this endeavor, birding, I knew I had a lot to learn and wasn't afraid to seek advice from people more experienced. Perhaps it's a maturity I learned during this period where I continued to self-reflect and soul search. Maybe I came to that conclusion subconsciously. Nevertheless, I didn't always have this mentality. The second lesson from the fishing example is this: advisors and coaches can come in all shapes and sizes, including 10-year-old boys. Thanks, Johnny. I owe you a couple cold ones. In 10 years.

Back to the birds. Birds like my fishing buddy, the Great Blue Heron, provided a nice "entry-level" experience as I began this new hobby. The Great egret, which is the species in the photograph used to start this chapter, is another one, and I bring him up again because, not only did I find early success taking photos of Egrets, whenever I was with Dylan and Noah during our adventures, and they asked me if they could try to take a photo, my immediate reply was, "Yes, of course, but let's wait until we see an egret or something."

This allowed them to focus on their subject long enough to be able to get a good photograph with my camera, which can be a tad difficult to do with certain birds and next to impossible if they were trying to shoot something buzzing around that refused to sit still. An egret or a heron is the closest thing they'd be able to shoot that was essentially immobile, almost like a plant or flower. If I had them try on something I found challenging even, I knew it most likely would be discouraging for them and be a deterrent for trying again anytime soon.

It was not just the big wading birds that allowed me to gain confidence and experience, though. Even species such as the Northern Mockingbird, which incidentally is the Florida State Bird, as well as Blue Jays, Doves, Red-bellied Woodpecker, and, yes, even Cardinals, are relatively easy to photograph once you start to look for them.

One reason why this is the case, as I later learned, is since these birds are year-round locals, they are more familiar, and, also, more comfortable with their surroundings, given it's their natural habitat. And, even if they don't know *me* personally, they are also comfortable because they encounter humans like me often enough to know I am not a threat.

I recently made the comment to a gentleman I met through one of the birding groups I belong to that, "It's actually a good thing I didn't start this when these warblers started to show up for fall migration. I'd have tried to photograph one, become annoyed when I couldn't, then never attempt it again." Just as it happened seven years ago after my unsuccessful attempt at fishing. He laughed and agreed that "They do make it tough, don't they?" And that is part of the fun. Now. But had I started with this sort of a challenge, chances are I would have thrown in the towel and said, "this sh*t is for the birds."

I joked with my mom during one of our more recent walks at Plantation Preserve as I was looking for hard-to-find warblers hiding in trees, including—the second species mentioned in this title's chapter—Ovenbirds. When we first started visiting the trail in May, I probably spent 90 percent of my time looking out at the water for the Egrets and Limpkins, but I don't think I even looked at the water once on that visit. The Ovenbird was one of the birds I was looking for that day. And the reason why I felt the need to clarify that I wasn't "talkin' turkey," is because, like many others that I've since seen and photographed, it is also one that I hadn't heard of before this past August. If I were to have heard the term Ovenbird before then, I would envision the type of ovenbird that we cover in a deluge of gravy, mashed potatoes, and stuffing every fourth Thursday in November.

But, no, Ovenbirds are songbirds and members of the New World warbler family, and even though they are among the larger of the warblers, they can be among the toughest to be seen, oftentimes on the ground and somewhat hidden under trees. They can be even tougher to photograph because their brownish coloring blends in with the dirt, brush, and the leaves where they are most spotted. Even the most experienced birders have some trouble with them. This is why I chose it for the title of this chapter, along with the egret.

In fact, the gentleman I mentioned above, Bruce, the day I made that comment to him is the day we coincidentally were at the same park in Coral Springs, a city on the northern side of Broward about 20 minutes from me. We ended up chatting and walked together for a few minutes. That day he was searching for an Ovenbird at the earliest stages of fall migration. We both saw one, my first, but the bird never came anywhere close enough for either of us to attempt a photograph.

Thus, had I been on the hunt for an Ovenbird during my first-ever outing, not only would I have not been able to photograph one—just as I hadn't been able to that late August morning either—but I likely would not have been able to even see one. I would not have, at that early point, been looking for other clues and signs that I will discuss in later chapters, because I wouldn't know that I needed to yet. I'd have gone home, not only photo-less, but also discouraged that I didn't see anything and wasn't "good" at this new hobby.

I'll clarify now that anyone can become good at birding. All it takes is some positivity, and as I dive into in future chapters— some patience, persistence, and perseverance, among other things. But equally important, you must give yourself the benefit of knowing you have to learn some things first before you will be "good" at it.

This is a lesson that is applicable to any new endeavor you embark upon, either personal or professional. In fact, in today's environment, it may be *the* most important in the sense that many people nowadays may be finding themselves starting a new job because of the events of the last few months. For instance, much like your kids who had to adjust to a new way of learning with virtual technology, you may be starting a new job in a new industry and find yourself frustrated and discouraged if you don't "get it" right away, especially if you haven't had to necessarily learn something new on the professional front in quite some time.

We're not supposed to get it right away. Just like babies cannot be expected to walk right away, either. In such a fast-paced world where we are always on the go and always on the move, we seldom take the opportunity to pause and tell ourselves it's okay for something to seem unfamiliar. We will not be an expert overnight. But if we give ourselves the benefit of taking the time needed to ramp up, soon enough we will be.

It is also important that we celebrate and acknowledge some early wins we have while we're learning something new. Take the time to recognize ourselves and understand that each small success ultimately leads to a much greater success and a bigger reward over time. Depending on the endeavor, this may come after a few months or longer, or it may come after a few days. It's important to set the right expectations, regardless.

I mentioned above, children adjusting to online learning. I think we take for granted our kids' resilience sometimes, and here's an example. On the very first day of school, my first-grade daughter, Emma, the perfectionist, became easily frustrated when she couldn't figure out certain prompts on her video conference, such as unmuting her microphone. I watched as she beat herself up the first couple days as she tried to grasp new technology that I never in a million years had to worry about trying to master when I was six years old. I think my first-grade curriculum included lessons on how to tie our shoelaces, so becoming fluent in the Microsoft Office Suite was clearly not a concern.

Emma was upset and since she is also naturally shy, was

somewhat reluctant to ask her teacher for help. "Dad, I can't do this," she would say through tears in her eyes, but also with a bit of an edge, too, because it was equal parts anger at herself as it was feeling defeated about not understanding the program. "Yes, you can," I reassured her. "But guess what? Even if you can't now, you will learn. That is why you are in school. If you knew it all, you wouldn't be there, right?"

By the second week of school, I heard her from the other room, muting and unmuting her mic and thus confidently participating. If I even dared to pop in to check on her, she shooed me away as if to say, "Dad, I got this." (Which I loved and hated at the same time). My words to Emma are a good reminder for all of us, and, I would say, the most important part is what I said after I reassured her that she can do it. Which is, even if she can't now, she will know how to soon enough.

I think we put a lot of pressure on ourselves to know "it" right now. We shouldn't put those types of expectations on ourselves. Another thing to keep in mind is, we also have to be mindful to take note of the progress we make as we're on our way to learning or mastering a new "thing." While Emma's gratification came fairly quickly, this is not always the case.

Throughout my career, I've led and supported major projects for organizations from a change management perspective. Many of the projects had a finish line that was a year away if not more.

We were asking a lot of employees, knowing that they wouldn't reach that finish line for many, many months, to give it a lot of time, effort, and adjustments. They'd have to do a lot of it without seeing the pay-off for their hard work until some point in the distant future, thus we had to celebrate milestones along the way, to give people the sense of accomplishment and a taste of success needed to obtain the confidence to continue their journey. Going back to the story with Noah and his piano—he had to learn *Twinkle, Twinkle Little Star* before he could learn *Ode to Joy* or anything written by Billy Joel.

As I close this chapter, I'll share that the day I was with my mom in September looking for an Ovenbird, I did get a photograph of one. Another milestone to celebrate in the journey, and another reminder that continuous progress comes only if we allow ourselves to first understand that we won't get there overnight.

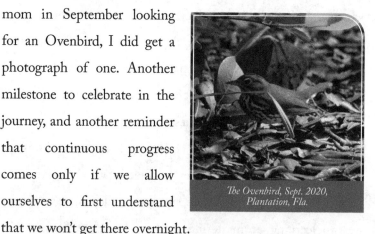

The Ovenbird, Sept. 2020, Plantation, Fla.

Remember then, even as adults, we must allow ourselves the chance to crawl before we walk. And, to look for Egrets before we go chasing that Ovenbird.

Chapter 3

PATIENCE, PERSISTENCE, AND PERSEVERANCE: THE SPOT-BREASTED ORIOLE AND...SOMETHING THAT MAY BE AN ORIOLE

"Matt, why don't you just go back tonight? You'll stew all night otherwise."— My Wife, Kristie

— My Mother, Ruth

The Spot-breasted Oriole taken June 2020, Markham Park, Sunrise, Florida.

Are you one of those people, if you're observing someone struggle to complete a routine task, within seconds of watching, you ask if you can take a crack at it? Say, opening a stubborn jar of pickles that won't budge or untangle a necklace that looks part of a recovered shipwreck? Or asking to help complete a crossword puzzle where one clue in particular leaves the other person stumped? And you know, if *you* were doing that puzzle, you'd get the answer in no time.

Then, when that person reluctantly lets you try—reluctantly of course, because they want to do it themselves—you struggle. And then, when they ask for it back after it becomes clear you haven't "cracked the code" nor appear to be close to doing so anytime soon, you refuse? And insist that, "I got it. Just give me a second, will you please?"

Even if you sit there all night, that chain will become unknotted one way or another. You might have to watch videos and scour the internet for tips. It may even require the use of "tools" that others have found useful as "life hacks." Regardless, one thing is for certain—you will get that dang thing untangled. If you're one of those people, then you're probably nodding along, perhaps imagining yourself at the kitchen table in the wee hours of the night, like MacGyver, trying to untangle a necklace with screwdrivers and Q-tips, and duct tape, always duct tape.

I mentioned earlier that my kids play video games. If I

walk by the television and see Dylan playing a baseball game, I'll channel my inner gamer and say, "Let me take a swing." It may take a batter or two, which will result in Dylan getting fidgety in his seat, but I'll get it and then nonchalantly toss the controller back to Dylan—with a subdued celebration because it wasn't a matter of *if* but *when*, so no need to go overboard—and go on about my day. Yep, still got it.

This is where having a penchant for persistence and perseverance pays off and what this chapter is all about. Because, as you might suspect, having what I'd call a stubborn confidence that drives you to persist and persevere can make a huge difference in your birding endeavors, especially if you don't taste success the first time you attempt to see a bird you are pursuing and trying to photograph.

A lot of times, this sense of stubbornness has a negative connotation, and it does have its drawbacks if you're not mindful of when you allow it to blind yourself to the point of not knowing when to stop and change course. But, when held in check, holding on to the belief that if you just give yourself a few more chances to get it right before you move on, then that can lead to success you otherwise may not have realized without that sense of confidence. Without that little piece of you saying to yourself, "I got this. Let's try it one more time."

Here is a story and lesson on how persistence and

perseverance paid off for me early in my birding adventures. One day, in early June, the boys and I were at another park that I had wanted to visit—and in truth, we were not there that day for birding. It was another gem just 10 minutes from me, Markham Park in Sunrise. It boasts campgrounds, mountain bike trails, fishing spots, boat ramps, picnic areas, a dog park (Barkham Park—how cute is that?), and even a target range. They also have one of the region's top spots for flying Remote Control Airplanes.

Emma stayed back, so it was just the boys. We brought our gloves and a couple baseballs and threw it around for a little bit. This place is massive, but we ended up over by the campgrounds area because it provided great views of the waterways that ran along the park on State Road 84, where boats and jet skis zoomed by on occasion.

It was great. Just the three of us throwing the baseball on a warm summer afternoon in Florida, laughing and goofing around. I always try to invent new games and challenges to keep things fresh. Like behind the back catches or seeing if I can throw the ball with enough accuracy so the boys don't have to move their glove to catch it. And variations of "try not to drop it" challenges and the like. We had a good time but decided to call it a day and head home for an afternoon swim after an hour or so. Because, when I said it was a warm summer afternoon, that was my attempt at seeing the glass half full, if you remember that from earlier. Truth be told, it was hot. Very hot. So, a quick trip to the store for some Gatorades followed by a dip in the pool would round out the afternoon's agenda.

We headed back to the car. As I was getting in the driver side, I saw something orange and black dart by me in a flash. At this point, just a few weeks into birding, I had already made significant progress being able to identify certain species. A big leap from my first outing when I took a picture of a Limpkin without even knowing what a Limpkin was. No, by this point, there were a few I could pick out of a line-up if necessary and one was the Spot-breasted Oriole. I wasn't entirely sure this was one, but I had a feeling it might have been for a couple reasons. For one, it quickly became one of my "must-sees," after I read a week or two earlier in the *Birds of Florida,* "Birders throughout North America visit the Fort Lauderdale, Miami and West Palm Beach areas, searching for Spot-breasted Oriole."

So, when I went to Markham that day, it was not with the intention of seeing any birds, let alone one that entices people from all over the country to come to Florida. But after the suspected Oriole zoom by me, I got into my car a little shocked, and despite having great time with the kids, I'll be honest, I was a tad peeved I missed a great opportunity to try to snap a photo. I wasn't discouraged because, it can be easy to get discouraged if you're not successful after a first attempt. In this case, I didn't even get an attempt. So, no, I wasn't discouraged. Instead of discouragement, it was determination I felt as we pulled out, as I thought to myself, "I'll just come back tomorrow at the same time and get a photo then."

The next day, at the same time, we went back to Markham Park, only this time I had my camera in hand. We headed over to the same area by the campgrounds and I waited there for a few minutes. In the meantime, I heard the

The Monk Parakeet. June 2020. Sunrise, Fla.

unmistakable sound of what are commonly referred to as the Wild Green Parrots of South Florida. In actuality, there are a variety of species of green parakeets that make up these green parrots and I had already seen two: The Blue-Crowned and Mitred Parakeets. They are always a treat, and yes, very, very loud. But seeing any that day was another case of luck and "right place, right time" as a flock of Monk *Parakeets* provided dozens of fun photo opportunities as I waited for the Oriole to emerge. Monk Parakeets had been on my "must-see" list too, by the way.

After about 10 minutes of hanging with the parrots, low and behold, a Spot-breasted Oriole flew by, but this time I had my camera. Got one! I watched as he landed in a nearby tree. I hustled over there, knowing he could dart off again any second. I got a little closer and managed to snap one more photo before he took off. I was about to try to follow him again…but then the skies opened like they sometimes do in the middle of summer, with no warning. Downpour. I was okay, though, because I got my two photos, plus some great ones of the Monk Parakeets. I drove home drenched, but again, not discouraged. I was happy to get the two photos and anxious to see how they turned out.

I got home and uploaded my photos. The ones of the Monk Parakeets included some real gems, including some of them snacking and a few of them making funny eye contact with me. Now, to check on the two Oriole photos. First, the one of him flying by. Yeah, not great. I got a photo, but I can do better. It was just a little blurry and the lighting not very good. It wasn't exactly a strike out. But it wasn't a home run either. The second one wasn't much better. Because I was concerned that he would fly off if I got any closer, I took it from a further vantage point than I wanted. I guess if I had waited to get closer before I took one, then I wouldn't have gotten one at all. Either way, a little better, but not great. Maybe a long fly ball, but still not a home run.

Let me add there is some debate about how much getting a good photo matters, and the consensus is, there is no consensus. It is very much a personal thing, and for me, getting a good photo to serve as a souvenir or keepsake of each memorable sighting is just as important as the sighting itself. Some would rather have the memory only and that's fine, too. But I want the photos. And what I had of the Oriole, so far, weren't quite good enough.

So, I went back to the park after dinner. Kristie thought I was a tad nuts, but she also knew if I didn't go after mentioning how I wanted to, that I'd stew about the house thinking about it all night. And she was probably right. So, she sent me on my way. At that time of the summer, it was still light out and I knew exactly where I was headed and knew I had about 30-45 minutes of decent enough light to try and make it happen. No luck. He wasn't there and I'd leave the park once again even more determined.

The next day, which if you're keeping track was my third attempt (fourth time back at the park in three days if you include the time I was there playing baseball but, hey, I was out of work, in case you forgot). After about 10 minutes, back at the same location, and yes, more Monk Parakeets, too, without warning—like the thunderstorm the previous day—not one, not two, but three Spot-breasted Orioles emerged. I took several photos. They flew to other nearby trees. I followed them, took some more. I couldn't believe it. I took at least 20.

A juvenile, which I hadn't read about, had a lighter, yellowish color. The adult male, which I figured out was the one I had seen the previous two days was bright, rich with orange and striking black feathers. The third turned out to be an adult female, also a tad on the lighter side and almost a yellowish color.

They are among my favorite photos that I've taken thus far, not only for the beauty of the birds themselves, but because they remind me of the importance of persistence and perseverance. And that things might not be as easy as we want them to be. But by maintaining just a little bit of a stubborn confidence that I was capable of better, I was able to achieve a result that left me feeling gratified. I will add that since that day, I've seen several more Orioles—at Markham and other places—including a surprise visitor to my backyard (pictured here). And each time I do, it provides a similar feeling as it did the first time that I saw one dart by as I was unsuspectingly walking to my car after a game of catch with the boys.

So, that's my story on perseverance and persistence but you may have noticed a third P word in the title of this chapter: Patience. Often, you will hear the terms perseverance, persistence, and  patience all used together. When I first had the idea to write this book, I had them as separate chapters, with patience being its own, but I chose to combine them for a couple reasons. For one, it's because I do think the three of them go hand in hand. And two, while I believe the ability to demonstrate persistence and perseverance is something I've been able to do throughout my life, patience has not always been an equal part of the pie. Thus, if you want to consider perseverance, persistence, and patience as a three-legged stool, let's just say, one of the three legs on my stool would be significantly shorter than the other two.

A lesson I learned a few weeks later taught me patience and is also one of the biggest factors in finding success at birding. It came courtesy of another bird that, as the title of this chapter states, might have been an Oriole also. At the end of the day, birding can be nothing more than an exercise in patience. This won't come as news to anyone who has been at this a while, but this has proven to be one of the top lessons I have learned thus far, and one I have already been able to transfer into other real-life situations. While I tend to let my stubbornness drive my ability to persevere, in this story I am about to tell, the need to demonstrate patience was forced upon me by the bird I was attempting to view versus my own sense to be patient or natural inclination to demonstrate it.

In late August, I made my first visit to another park on my summer list: Richardson Historic Park and Nature Preserve in Fort Lauderdale. Within my first few minutes there, I had already seen a number of species, including, coincidentally more Spot-breasted Orioles. As I made my way to the boardwalk area to explore that area of the park, something caught my eye. I didn't know what it was but at first glance maybe, this too, was some kind of Oriole? I snapped a photograph but knew there would be no way of knowing for sure based on this one photo alone as I previewed it through my camera's preview screen. I wasn't satisfied with this uncertainty. Also, unlike the Oriole, which I knew was a year-round resident, I was not sure what this bird even was, so I figured the only way to know for sure, or at least try to know, was to wait it out, right then and there. So, I stood there in the same spot. And stood there some more.

Finally, after about 10-15 minutes (if I had to guess) he emerged again from behind the dense foliage. I knew he was back there, I should add, which is why I decided to stay in the same spot. So, in this specific instance, it really was just a matter of time, because at some point, he'd have to pop out. And once he did, I'd be there, ready for him. So, after patiently waiting, I watched as he jumped to another set of branches, only this time, one that allowed me to clearly see him and photograph him at relatively close range. And, fortunately, which is not always the case with these smaller and faster birds, he remained visible long enough for me to get a half dozen great shots.

When I got home, I uploaded my photos, feeling excited but still not knowing what this bird was. Even though I saw him up close, this was also at the start of fall migration and my familiarity with all the new arrivers was still not that strong and for some reason, this was one I hadn't remembered reading about in any of my books.

It turned out, after looking at some of the books, as well as a quick search to compare to other pictures online to confirm, this striking and remarkable bird was a male American Redstart, a member of the New World warbler family. And as was the case with the Orioles, a bird I have continued to see over the last few months, even if that first time he tested my patience like no other bird had before.

On the previous page is a collage, where you can see that first photo I reference, and why I was not satisfied with the lack of confirmation! In case you are wondering why I made the point to call out that this was a male, it's because female American Redstarts are a mix of yellow, white, and grey. Neither of them, by the way, appear to have any "red" in them.

That story is the experience that taught me the lesson on patience. And this is how would I then describe the relationship between perseverance and persistence and patience. I see **perseverance** as having the determination and **persistence** to keep going, day after day, until you've reached your goal and feel satisfied with your results. It is **patience** that allows yourself to remain calm and poised, and not become flustered when those satisfying results take a little longer to come into focus, while also giving yourself the time to know good things come to those who wait.

Patience is also the ability to know when you still have

some crawling to do, or maybe I should say, walking before you begin to run. Patience is also what allows me to understand that I am several years, at least, away from being able to accomplish other loftier goals as it relates to birding or otherwise, and that's okay. If it is something I feel passionately about, I will eventually get there. Persistence and perseverance will drive me; patience is what will allow me to take my time without feeling the need to hurry or rush before I am ready to. More on passion next chapter.

Since I am on the topic of patience and admitted that this was not something that I considered a strength before—perhaps not even before the American Redstart sighting in August—I have found myself already being able to apply it in other areas of my life. I won't go as far as to say, I'll be able to sit in bumper-to-bumper traffic for hours at a time without moving an inch, with a big old smile on my face but I will, at least, have the perspective to ask myself, "What's the hurry anyway?"

For a parent, child, sibling, boss, colleague, coach, friend, spouse, spouse (yes, I said that twice on purpose!), and of course birder, patience will pay dividends over and over throughout your life. Not only for the others you interact with, but more importantly, for yourself.

I stumbled upon an article through the University of California, Berkley, that revealed that patient people enjoy better mental and physical health, and, not surprisingly, are more likely to achieve their goals in life.

While I still have to continue to work on being mindful to remain patient, even when it doesn't always come natural to, I am already seeing the payoff. It certainly helped me find the American Redstart. And that's a (red)start.

Chapter 4

PASSION: THE ROSEATE SPOONBILL

"Dad, I have my piano lesson today."

— My Son, Noah

The Roseate Spoonbill taken June 2020 at Arthur R. Marshall Loxahatchee National Wildlife Refuge, Palm Beach County, Florida.

Ever drive through your neighborhood and see a young kid shooting baskets in his driveway, even in the pouring rain? He'll stand out there all night, attempting the same shot again and again, as if Game Seven of the NBA Finals would someday come down to him making that same game-winning shot that he's been practicing for hours on end.

That is passion. When you find yourself enjoying something so much, you want to keep doing it and push yourself to keep getting better, too. Not because you *have* to but because you *want* to.

I said in the earliest pages of this book, that throughout my life I've had many interests and hobbies. I also said that not all of them turned into passions. Sometimes they would, and sometimes they wouldn't. In general, I believe that when these hobbies do become passions, more often than not we don't necessarily see it coming. So, maybe then it's because the passion chooses us.

You may have observed that I've shared a couple sports-related stories about my older son, Dylan, and a piano-related story about my younger, son, Noah. He, too, has played sports, including baseball and flag football. In a normal fall, he'd be playing flag football as I type these words. He has fun playing. But he's not *passionate* about it. Piano on the other hand, seems to be, sort of like the nature trails were for me last summer, somewhat of a sanctuary for Noah.

Like many kids his age, sometimes Noah can be a little "all over the place" on a given day, but as soon as he sits down at the piano and starts to play, it's as if somehow all his energy is channeled into playing those keys. Julie, his teacher, once told him during a recent lesson—now done via FaceTime—he has "magical hands." High praise from a classically trained pianist with a PhD. Now, perhaps, you have a better understanding of why I was confident in his ability to play a Billy Joel song.

I'll be honest, it's not always my favorite thing, if I am sitting in the living room where the piano is, trying to read a book (or write one), and he'll pop in and start playing, but I never (or rarely) stop him. I wouldn't want to dampen his passion inadvertently by discouraging him to play. The fact that he plays on his own, without having to be reminded to "practice," is, in fact, a sign of his passion for playing.

Conversely, Dylan took piano lessons at one point in his life, and if memory serves, because he's two years older, he may have taken them first, before Noah began playing. Either way, he doesn't play anymore, and hasn't since he got into travel baseball a little over a year ago because there wasn't enough time. For him, the reason is irrelevant: he's just happy he's not playing anymore. He didn't dislike the piano, it's just that, again, it's not his passion. And, so, oftentimes when it came time to have to sit down and practice, he looked at it as a chore rather than an outlet to fuel his inherent passion. Dylan is passionate about sports, all of them, and like many kids (I grew up with one, in fact), he is driven by a passion to not only play them but play them well and succeed. Everyone likes to win—Dylan needs to.

In the fall of 2019, when they were both playing flag football, both happened to have teammates whose parents took photos of the games. I have done this in the past, but it's always nice when there  is someone on the team talented enough, and willing, to take photos and videos of all the kids, not just their own, and share them with the other parents.

It's incredible that, most likely without even realizing it, the two photographers / parents who took and then shared with me these two photos on the right, both somehow managed to capture my sons' truest and sincerest personalities in terms of how each approach playing sports.

In looking at the way they each play, one must appreciate the juxtaposition here. Just a smidge of difference in their facial expressions and even their body language. Dylan, on the left, looks as though he'd rather run you over than stop to exchange hellos. Call it intensity, call it determination but whatever you want to call it, it's fueled by his passion for the sport, and, like I said, for winning. While one could argue Noah actually looks like he's enjoying himself more than Dylan is, he is just having fun and is happy to be running the ball. If you didn't know any better, you may even assume it is Noah with the passion for sports based on that smile.

But the look on your face isn't always a tell-tale sign of passion. You can enjoy something and have fun doing it without being passionate about it. On the other hand, that look of intensity and determination, like the one on Dylan's face, would not otherwise be there if you weren't driven by a passion to play the game—any game or any sport—at the highest level you're capable of playing it. There's an old baseball movie with Kevin Costner, no, not *Field of Dreams*, called *For Love of the Game*. Sure, I suppose one can rise to the ranks of the Major Leagues simply fueled by their love of baseball, but my suspicion is, their passion for winning, for the pursuit of being able to excel at the highest level, is actually what got them there. Even with natural talents, it requires a passion to continue to put in the grueling hours it takes to reach that level to ever reach it.

Going back to my above statement, it's not always up to us to choose our passions, it's the passions that choose us, and I believe this is a good example. Therefore, both of my sons have taken piano lessons and have been exposed to all kinds of sports throughout their childhood. And the reason is because, again, we wanted them to find their passion on their own, whether through sports or through music, or something completely different if it came to it.

I know lots of parents, fathers in particular, who—how do I put this—have rather strong opinions when it comes to their sons playing sports. For the most part, I believe this comes from a well-meaning place. For example, I have a friend whose son is much younger than mine are, but our daughters are around the same age, and we met up at a neighborhood park one day with all the kids. Dylan, Noah, and I were tossing the baseball around at one point, and he made the comment that he couldn't wait until the days where he, too, can play catch with his son. What father doesn't *dream* of this sort of thing? (Dream in italics because how could you not picture the tear-jerking scene from *Field of Dreams* when thinking about a father-son catch? There's the Kevin Costner baseball movie you wanted me to mention).

And that's great. However, I also know fathers who quickly let that desire turn into more of a mandate. Another guy I've become friendly with down here, who once had a son on one of Dylan's teams, said to me a couple years ago, "I'd make my son play baseball even if he didn't want to. Even if he hated it."

His kid *did* want to play so who knows how serious he was since he was speaking rather hypothetically. Come to think of it, he said this to me in response to me telling him that I wasn't sure if I would be signing Noah up that spring because he had just started piano and had also expressed an interest in Karate as well. So, in looking back, he almost said it with a hint of judgment—like what father *wouldn't* want his kid to play baseball? Of course, I wanted him to play, and I encouraged him to as well.

As I said, my little league days are among the happiest memories of my childhood, so why wouldn't I want Noah to be able to experience those same sorts of memories, too? But if he did truly hate it, and, no, that wasn't the case but *if* he did then, no, I wouldn't make him play. I also would realize that his childhood memories might include the day he nailed his piano guild audition, or the day he performed Billy Joel for his old man instead. I did end up signing Noah up for baseball that year, by the way, but the following year he took the spring off for Karate. He can always play again next season, if he wants.

But my friend's statement is a tad interesting, and I am not suggesting that all parents need to parent a certain way. But, for me, I think there is a fine line between encouraging your kids to play a certain sport—especially for the valuable lessons youth sports teach us, such as teamwork, camaraderie, discipline, how to accept defeat (a lesson most adults still struggle with), etc.— and forcing them to play a certain sport because *you* want them to, perhaps solely based upon your own passion for the sport yourself.

Certainly, as I said, we signed the kids up for anything and everything, especially when they were younger, and didn't give them much of a say in the matter. My boys took tennis lessons at one point, for example, and, as I shared earlier, golf. So, yes, when they are at a younger age, we have to make the call as parents what we sign them up for and what we expose them to. But it should all be done through the lens of helping them find out what their true passion is. And, once they find it, encourage it, nurture it, and invest in it *with* them and *for* them. But the idea of forcing your kid to play a sport that they don't enjoy— or to use the words from my friend, one that they "hate"—after they have given it a chance, even if only for one season, seems a little misguided, even if it is through good intentions.

In case you're wondering about Emma, she has a passion for gymnastics and hip-hop dance. She took a ballet class through the same academy she now does hip-hop dance. (You should see this group of six-year-old girls performing in their costumes, but I digress). But she had no real interest in ballet. She likes to dance, but it was a different kind of dancing that brought out a different kind of spark that would turn into a passion for her.

Thus, while you can make the case that we can develop a

passion for a certain hobby or activity over time, there are some passions that already exist within us, and they are just waiting there to be discovered. And, sometimes, we stumble upon them unknowingly. I once heard the phrase, though even after researching it to use in this book, I cannot seem to find an author to attribute it to, but the phrase is, "The best way to get a good idea is to have a lot of ideas." In that same vein, the best way to find your passion for a particular hobby is to try a lot of hobbies.

As it relates to developing passions, yes, that can happen, too. In using some of the lessons I already shared, this can come by giving yourself time to learn it (i.e., crawling before you walk), tasting some success, gaining some confidence, and then realizing you want more of it. So there obviously is something to be said about having your kid give baseball, for example, two seasons or, maybe, even three, to see if something stronger develops. Certainly, it's reasonable to say that you must give yourself, or your kids, the time to see something through before you know if there is a passion there or not. And, if it's not there, it also doesn't mean you have to pull them from the team, because, like I said, you can participate in, and even enjoy, a particular activity without having a passion for it.

If you hate it, or it interferes with your ability to pursue your true passions (because of time commitments, for instance), then at some point you'll have to decide when to cut something out. At one point in time, William Shakespeare had to stop trying to split atoms to write *Romeo and Juliet* and Albert Einstein gave up on authoring the next great tragedy before he moved on to tackling the theory of relativity.

Noah walking over to the piano to start playing (even at inopportune times), Emma trying to perform gymnastics stunts on my living room furniture, and Dylan going out into the backyard to toss the ball to himself or hit baseballs into a net, are all examples of passions taking over to the point you find yourself wanting to do it whenever, and wherever, you can.

The first time I realized birding was becoming a passion was the first time I ventured outside of Broward to look for something unfamiliar. It seems almost silly in hindsight because, as you'll read in later chapters, traveling to places outside my own area in pursuit of a different bird has now become commonplace for me. But the first time I did so is what made me realize the difference between casual interest and passion. It's one thing to spend an hour at the Plantation Preserve trail, with my mom, five minutes from my home, walking and chatting and looking for birds. It's another thing to drive an hour, almost to the point of inconveniencing myself, to look for a specific bird that I might not even see. This is when you know something is more than just a casual hobby. And so, this is the story of the Roseate Spoonbill.

By mid-June, when I wasn't birding, I was already finding myself reading books (at that point I had a few, and have since ordered more), engaging in discussions online, and simply immersing myself into this new world as often as it would allow, while not ignoring my other responsibilities and hobbies that are still important. Like building Legos with the kids, for example, and continuing to pursue new career opportunities, too, of course. But, when I had "me" time at the end of the evening, when others were asleep, rather than watch television, I'd find myself browsing through one of my bird books instead.

That's when I stumbled upon the Roseate Spoonbill, something that almost looks as though it came out of a Lewis Carol novel. With its bright pink plumage, long spoon-shaped flat bill, and bald white head, this bird is among the most majestic, if not magical looking, of all of the species that can be seen in Florida. As mentioned, though, it was like many I'd want to find later that summer, not in Broward, at least not commonly enough for me to visit a specific place in the county to see one with any probability.

There are other places in the state of Florida where they are commonly found, sometimes dozens at a time. The most well-known of these places is on the west coast of the state, in Sanibel, called J.N. Ding Darling National Wildlife Refuge. I've wanted to visit Sanibel for a long time, since moving to Florida, in fact. It's only about two hours and change away, but we haven't been there yet, for one reason or another. We actually had plans to go there last summer, over Labor Day weekend, but a potential hurricane was expected to make landfall that weekend, too. So, we decided to postpone it. My mother has been a couple times and it is known for having seashell beaches where seashell collectors will feel like kids in a candy shop. She's come home with sand dollars, too.

So, yes Sanibel is on the list. And it's actually for that reason why I would choose not to venture there in search of the Roseate Spoonbill. Driving two hours each way isn't totally unreasonable for me. I've done trips to Walt Disney World, three hours away, there and back in the same day, plenty of times. So that wasn't why. It's because if we were going to visit Sanibel, I'd want to do it the right way, for a long weekend with the entire family, and when we could take advantage of all it had to offer, which we wouldn't be able to do for several more months, at least.

Instead, I chose to head somewhere a little closer, one county north, for what would become my first of many visits to Palm Beach County in search of new additions to my "lifer" list, specifically to Arthur R. Marshall Loxahatchee National Wildlife Refuge about 45 minutes from my home.

The three kids and I piled into the van and made our way northbound in search of something cool and new. When we arrived, we headed over to the Marsh Trail and immediately saw some other firsts for me, such as the Purple Gallinule, the Little Blue Heron, and a family of Sandhill Cranes that looked as though they were just out for a leisurely family stroll. They walked right by us in the opposite direction, without so much as seeming even remotely concerned by our presence.

We made our way along the trail, and Emma and Noah were excited to discover this place had an observation tower that they turned into their "treehouse" for the next 10 minutes or so as Dylan and I looked around for the Spoonbill. If you're wondering why I didn't use the observation tower to look, I did. But I didn't see one, so I came down. I was able to keep an eye on them though as I looked around other parts of the marsh.

Then, suddenly, there he was by himself, a bright pink Roseate Spoonbill with his bill plunging in and out of the water, either taking a drink or, like the Great Blue Heron I mentioned in an earlier chapter, looking for something to eat. He stood there in the same spot as I took what must have been 50 photos. In carrying the lesson over from earlier in this book, the Roseate Spoonbill exercised as much patience as a Great Egret in terms of letting me have my own private photo shoot with him.

The photoshoot, though, had to come to somewhat of an abrupt halt and we high tailed it home once I realized it was Wednesday and it meant Noah had his piano lesson. Normally, for whatever reason, "Field Trip Day" was a Tuesday, so I hadn't realized it was even Wednesday. Sure enough, Noah was the one to remind me that he had a lesson and did just in time for us to leave and get home with only a couple minutes to spare. Noah being the one to remind me makes it more perfect.

There will be more times throughout this book where I offer to show my cell phone records because the stories and coincidences involved in some of them have such a serendipitous quality to them. This is one. How will my cell records help? Because just in case I hit unexpected traffic, I texted Noah's teacher, Julie, to let her know he may be five or so minutes late and I took total responsibility for it, if so. Rushing home from my passion so Noah could get home in time for his—these things cannot be scripted.

The Roseate Spoonbill remains my favorite of the birds I've photographed. When I decided to make an online album on Facebook later in the summer, I chose the same photo used for the title page of this chapter, as the cover image of that album, and it's still the cover image. It serves as a reminder of the day I knew I had stumbled upon what likely would become a lifelong passion, not simply a way to pass time during a summer of unemployment. I still didn't know why it would be, but I knew that it most likely would be, regardless.

I have spent the entire chapter so far talking about passions from the perspective of hobbies and things we do outside of our professional lives. Passion, of course, plays a central part in our careers, too. Or, I should say, it can. I am aware that not everyone in the world has the luxury or opportunity to have a career that is based on one of their passions. I am certainly not suggesting that this is the only way to achieve the highest levels of success, either. But at the same time, you're likely not going to become the CFO of an organization if you weren't, at one point in time anyway, passionate about math. I almost said "math nerd" but didn't. But then I just did.

In today's environment, especially, I also am aware that if you've been out of work for a lengthy period, just as I was, you're likely not going to turn down a great job offer because it's not something you're passionate about. Please, if I were to suggest such a thing then I'd give you permission to stop reading this right now. No, I am not saying that. At all. But you could say that there might be elements of that job, or any job, that allows you to fuel your passions. You might have to look for them but sometimes having even one thing about your job that fulfills this need is more than enough to drive you to achieve great success.

This doesn't mean you have to love all parts of your job. Even jobs that are based on a passion, may include parts of it you don't love, but you "tolerate" them because of the pleasure you derive from the other parts. The parts that inspire you and fuel your passion, outweigh the parts that don't.

Oftentimes and back to the lesson on patience, it may take some time, but you might find it within your current company. I was having a conversation not too long ago with a colleague that had been with the company for 22 years. Like many people I've worked with, she was fortunate to have been able to explore different opportunities within the same company that allowed her to zero in on her passion. What makes her case even more interesting, but not surprising based on some of the themes I've discussed in this chapter, she stumbled on it unexpectedly, before she zeroed in on it.

And it started because in one of her earlier roles there was a minor training component involved, even though it wasn't the core focus of the role. She soon discovered though, this was what she liked most about it, then quickly developed a passion for it, and eventually found a position where training was not just a minor component of her role, but the main one. Like I said, it took her some time to do, but she was able to do it and has since enjoyed a career with longevity and fulfillment, too.

That's not to say my colleague ignored or overlooked the other responsibilities of her previous job but realizing that there were parts of it she liked more than others, it inspired her to consider pursuing a future opportunity within the company's formal training and development department. She might not otherwise have even considered it, had she not accidentally discovered her passion for instructional design and training delivery in an inadvertent way.

Jim Collins, the author of Good to Great, shares something he calls the Hedgehog Concept, which suggests that ultimate success is achieved based on three circles that all seamlessly and symmetrically intersect and include, "What you are deeply passionate about, what you can be the best in the world at, and what best drives your economic or resource engine."

Let me say that this is clearly a "utopian" view and an idealistic thing to achieve. I'll even take it down a notch and say, maybe not best in the world at, but good at—even great at, to use Collins' own words. For those fortunate to achieve this symmetry, who may be reading this, you'll likely agree that this might be the "secret formula" to your own success, without realizing it if, perhaps, you hadn't read Collins' book already. And, if you're sitting there, picturing Bobby Flay, for example, as the only type of person that this applies to, rest assured it's not the case. You do not need to be a celebrity chef, cookbook author, restaurateur, or one of the world's most talented culinary professionals who summers in the Hamptons, to achieve this three-criteria definition of success.

In many ways, I consider myself fortunate to have found this formula in my career, in nearly every role I've ever held. I've had jobs that allow me to fulfill my passion for writing, which I believe I am also good at—again, not suggesting in any way I am the best in the world at it, (maybe second best?)—and, yes, my career has allowed me to make a comfortable living and provide for my family, too.

Not all passions can be careers, and they're not supposed to be. If your greatest passion in life is cooking, then, yes, Bobby Flay's level of success could very well be right within your grasp. However, if your biggest passion is catching butterflies, you may want to research if it can "drive your economic engine," or at least pay your bills first. Otherwise, maybe do it on nights and weekends, like birdwatching.

Again, realizing this environment has provided challenging times for many and so any job at all is something for which to be grateful, on the flip side, this environment also reminds us to take the time to reassess what's most important, that sometimes we cannot put off for tomorrow what we should do today, and that sometimes life is indeed too short. So, if you have an opportunity to take the time to find those passions, whether personally or professionally, take it.

Also, bear in mind, sometimes the passions find us unexpectedly, when we don't even realize it. So, keep an open mind as you look for opportunities to potentially explore a new career path you hadn't thought of before. Maybe because you never allowed yourself the opportunity to slow down enough to consider them. Maybe because you never gave yourself permission to. Either way, give yourself that permission now, to keep an eye out for the opportunities in life that just might ignite a fire in you that fuels your passion in unexpected ways.

And keep an eye out for those Roseate Spoonbills, too. I've never seen anything quite like them. But, then again, I wasn't looking for one until this past summer, either.

Chapter 5

PUTTING IN TIME: THE YELLOW-CROWNED NIGHT HERON

"When is the book report due? Like next week?"— My Mother, Ruth

"Like, tomorrow."— Me

The Yellow-crowned Night Heron, taken May 2020 at Plantation Preserve Linear Trail, Plantation, Florida.

Throughout the last several chapters, I've alluded to this notion of "time." The importance of "putting in time" is a natural byproduct of essentially all lessons I've shared thus far: giving your yourself time to learn a new hobby before you attempt to tackle more complex tasks associated with it; allowing yourself to be patient enough to take the time to learn those things; and, certainly, once you find yourself passionate about a new hobby, you'll then end up wanting to put in the time to do it more often and get better at it, too.

So, this chapter is not about putting in time in that sense, because it's been covered and will continue to be covered to some extent in future chapters as well. Rather, this chapter is about the importance of putting in time as it relates to *each* task you set out to complete or each goal you attempt to achieve. One specific outing, that took place in the earliest days of my journey, is when I saw the bird that inspired this lesson, and another one, learned in hindsight. Because, as I would discover much later, it was a mistake. I'll explain more in a minute.

I am not embarrassed to admit I made mistakes along the way. I've shared some already, in fact. But that's okay. As is the case with most new hobbies, if not all, this is expected. Even Julia Child was driven to tears by her all-male classmates when she didn't know how to chop an onion on her first day of culinary school.

Not that I ever hope or expect to be compared to Julia Child, even if after watching Meryl Streep's charming performance of her in *Julie & Julia* made me want to cook my way through *Mastering the Art of French Cooking,* just like Julie Powell, the other title character in Nora Ephron's 2009 film did. The point here is that no one starts a new hobby knowing "all the tricks of the trade," even if they demonstrate a natural knack for being good at it. Tiger Woods famously appeared on *The Tonight Show* with Johnny Carson when he was four years old, and immediately put every middle-aged man in America to shame after one three-minute segment. But, 40 years later, he still has a swing coach for a reason, even after winning 15 major championships.

Mistakes are not only expected but, in fact, welcome. Whether you're aspiring to be a professional or, like I was, attempting to learn and spend time engaging in a newly found hobby, making mistakes early on shows that you are trying. It shows that you're willing to put yourself out there, even though it can be somewhat uncomfortable to do so. The important thing is being able to admit you made those mistakes, reflect on them, and then learn from them.

Here is one mistake I made that I mentioned above and serves as the basis for this chapter about the need to put in the time, *every time,* to get the results that you want.

After the outing on the morning of May 21 with my mom—the day of the Northern Cardinal experience at Plantation Preserve—I was then inspired to write and publish a blog on LinkedIn that ended up serving as the first in a series where I, for the first time, began sharing my perspective and insights about the journey I found myself on as an individual grappling with unemployment. In some ways, it was a journey that I knew many others were likely on as well. In that blog, when teeing up the story on the Northern Cardinal sighting, I made the innocent comment that, after the first time my mom and I visited the Preserve trail, "I found myself dropping by there, whenever I can, even if it's for about 10 minutes."

This included two times the previous weekend as I was on my way to Publix. On the second of those two occasions, a Sunday evening, as soon as I set foot on the trail, I immediately spotted what I later found out was a Yellow-crowned Night Heron. I saw him from behind, so I had to walk down a windy path a bit, off the path in fact, to be able to see his face and more of his body. He was dining on a catfish and was perhaps self-conscious about eating in front of strangers—at least one that appeared to be gawking and taking photos—so at one point he dropped it as if to say, "Go ahead, take a picture. I'll wait."

I snapped about six pictures and let the heron toward to his feast as I went back to my car before heading to the store on my way back home. So, 10 minutes, in hindsight, was a stretch. It was probably four or five. At this point, it wouldn't surprise me if you're thinking to yourself as you read this story, "I'm waiting for him to tell me why this is a bad thing or why he called it a mistake." Here's why. Because the sighting of the Yellow-Crowned Night Heron lulled me into a false sense of security, so to speak, and gave me perhaps the unrealistic expectation that it would *always* be that easy.

To cut myself some slack, it was an easy assumption to make, and at that point, likely a little too self-critical to call it a mistake. Back in those days, I used to have the goal of seeing at least one new bird every time I visited Plantation Preserve. This proved easy the first five or six times going because, even if I'd seen 15 birds my previous outing, there were still enough year-round resident species that finding a new one was not only possible, but probable. Not only was it a reasonable goal to set for myself, it was a fairly attainable one, too. And, in those very early days, such as the case with the Yellow-crowned Night Heron on my third-ever visit, attainable quickly, too. Back in those days, when I knew I didn't have a ton of time, I'd say to myself, "as soon as you see one new bird, leave." Again, reasonable.

One day, I was "pushing it" in terms of time. Stopping by the Preserve on my way to run another errand had, up to that point, been pretty much non-detectable. Not that I was hiding my birding endeavors or trying to get away with anything, but if Kristie asked me to run to the grocery store to pick up a gallon of milk, it might be hard to explain why that took 30 minutes. Not unlike Noah trying to play the piano just as I attempt to sit down and read a book in quiet, I, too, found myself trying to sneak in a quick birding trip, even at the most inopportune times. Like 6:00 p.m. on a Tuesday, and I had to run a quick errand before we sat down for dinner at 6:30.

So, on one of those occasions, I was pressing my luck, and I said to myself, as I walked in, "Okay, Matt, you have about 10 minutes, tops, so as soon as you see something new, get the heck outta dodge."

I walked in and saw all the usual suspects: egrets, mockingbirds, grackles, Blue Jays, Red-winged Blackbird.

A few more minutes: What's that? Oh, another White Ibis.

Two minutes later: Is that a….? Oh, it's just an Anhinga.

This would go on for a little longer until I realized that a 10-minute pit stop quickly turned into 20 and I still hadn't seen anything "new." I left, rushed to the store, and sped home, hoping no one would question the 30-minute trip to the store for two items.

Before I continue with the main lesson of this story and chapter, overall, I'll take a moment to address something I feel is important to clarify at this point. I've talked a lot about the fact that, oftentimes, it wasn't the birding itself that became my therapeutic escape last summer but the fact that I found myself almost lost in my own thoughts, while wandering through trails in what seemed like my own private parks, that helped me find this time for self-reflection. That is true, without question. So, I don't want to give the impression that my birding endeavors were 100 percent about getting in and out as quickly as I could, simply to add new birds to my personal checklist.

However, as with any new hobby, I did find myself, especially in the beginning, trying to log as much time as I could engaging in the hobby itself. The whole "get out after seeing one new bird" thing was my way of keeping myself in check when I knew that, as I said, I was pushing it in terms of sneaking in a visit when it wasn't exactly an ideal time to do so.

The other thing that I'll say is, noting that this was in the earliest days of my bird endeavors, I also hadn't realized at that point that the joy was in the pursuit, in the journey itself and the lessons I would learn while doing it. Which is what this book is about, of course, but it bears repeating from time to time throughout this book, that this light *bulb* was still light *years* away from going off (or is it on?). Either way, because all of this wouldn't become apparent to me until months later, it can be an easy thing to lose sight of as you read those earlier stories.

The Matt sneaking into Plantation Preserve in May on

his way to the store, is not the same Matt writing this book all these months later, let's put it that way, so I wanted to take that opportunity to make that reminder. I will still, on occasion, sneak in a few minutes at a park here and there. Only now my intentions for doing so are a little purer and more genuine because now it is about grabbing a few minutes of peace and solace amid the hecticness of life that matters most, not necessarily about padding my stats.

The last point I wanted to address as I share that story in hindsight, and I'll cover this in a later chapter, is I have since come to realize, that the "just an Anhinga" mindset was another mistake. I've come to not take for granted any of the species I see out there because they were and are all part of the overall journey. Again, I do have more thoughts on this concept I will dive deeper into later, but I didn't want to wait to make that clarification, too.

Back to the story. I got home that night, not feeling at all fulfilled, even after taking 20 minutes to enjoy my new hobby, but the more profound lesson on not appreciating the journey was not the reason why, again, not in those days. It was because it reinforced the importance on putting in time, in the simplest and most logical sense. Like, if it takes you an hour to mow your lawn, and you need to be finished by 5:00 p.m., it's probably not a good idea to start it at 4:30.

Sounds relatively basic but not really if you remember my comments in the opening pages about getting caught up in the hustle and bustle of life. Sometimes then, we really do only have 30 minutes for a lawn job that requires an hour. So, how do we reconcile that? I don't know, hire someone to mow your lawn, I guess? Why are you asking me?

The truth is, I don't know the answer to that, other than to say, we must do our best to focus on the ball that's about to hit the ground first, realizing we're juggling about 20 other balls at the same time. And the way to do that is to focus on that ball as soon as you can, once it enters the rotation. Simply put, to give ourselves a decent chance of meeting a goal, and ensuring that ball doesn't get dropped, we must give ourselves the time needed to do it within the context of everything else going on. The Yellow-crowned Night Heron is a great example of something we all need occasionally (certainly while out birding): luck. It's an exception to the rule, though, because showing up somewhere, giving it five to 10 minutes to complete something that would normally take 30 minutes, and still expecting success, is not the most prudent thing to do.

Look at it this way, if you had two hours to complete four tasks, allocated thirty minutes for each, and the last task was "see one new species tonight at Plantation Preserve," and you got there, realizing you only left yourself five minutes, instead of 30, to complete it, you might see one just like I did, but probably won't. That's the crux of this chapter and the lesson I was reminded of that day I ran to get bread and put too much pressure on myself to achieve a goal without enough time to do it.

Sometimes our cluttered schedules can be a key reason we don't allow ourselves this time to do something right, but a cluttered mind can as well. Sometimes all that clutter can make us overwhelmed to the point that we put off some of those tasks until we find ourselves with too little time, if any time at all, to get it done when the (bird) sh*t hits the fan.

When I was growing up, we always spent New Year's Day at my dad's parents' house—my YiaYia and Papou, may they their memories be eternal. I always had a love-hate relationship with those New Year's Day gatherings. College bowl games, an incredible feast (much better than that poor Night Heron's catfish), family, and savoring the last moments of the holiday season—what's not to love? Well, I just hinted at it. It signaled the last moments of the holiday season, and for kids, the end of winter break. Even as an adult, going back to work after a week or so of PTO during the holiday season is fairly tough if not slightly depressing. But, as a kid...well, it felt like the end of the world, not just the end of Christmas vacation, at least to me.

Perhaps it was out of denial, or maybe it was because I waited too long already, and, thus, I didn't know how to dig myself out of the hole I found myself in. But, as I stood there holding a shovel on New Year's Day, sometime back in the late 80s or early 90s—I honestly don't remember—I somehow gained the courage to tell my mom, as everyone else was enthralled in the Rose Bowl game on the big screen TV, that I had a book report due.

"When? Like next week?" she asked.

"Like tomorrow," I replied.

You know already that my mom's ever-present positive outlook on life is what allowed me to start seeing things last summer from a different perspective. Her heart emojis are like little rays of sunshine on a cloudy day. You can't help but feel better after spending even five minutes with my mother, and I know there are probably many other people in the world capable of emitting this type of infectious optimism into the universe. But those people aren't my mom.

On that fateful New Year's Day in 19-whatever it was, there were no heart emojis. There were no rays of sunshine. There was nothing emitting from my mom's soul that day other than a look in her eyes that makes me shiver to this very day. I was glad the shovel in my hand was only proverbial. She may have taken it from me and buried me in that hole I found myself standing in.

In truth, she handled it a million times better than I would have, and, hopefully, I'll never have to find out—knock on wood.

After saying our goodbyes and trying not to call attention to the fact our departure felt very abrupt, we hurried out of there faster than I did that day in Palm Beach County, rushing Noah home in time for piano. We got home, and with my mom's help, slapped together a book report that would at least be good enough for a passing grade. She could have let me do it alone, and perhaps that would have taught my 10-year-old, or however-old-I-was self, a harder lesson but, after all, my mother is more rainbow than rain cloud.

Still, this is a classic example of simply not giving myself the time needed to be successful. And in this case, which I've seen happen at various points throughout my life, it then creates somewhat of a snowball effect. If you put it off long enough, there reaches a point where you feel it's now too late to even start it, and then you become crippled by fear and yet that fear still doesn't translate into you finally rolling up your sleeves to get to work. It, as irrational as it seems, causes an opposite effect, until you finally reach the point where you have no other choice than to just finally stop the charade and do it.

In reality, it is always the dread of doing the work that is "scarier" than actually doing it. As long as it's not on the last day of winter break, and you are the reason your entire family had to leave in the middle of a big bowl game. Then, that's pretty darn scary, too.

This is quite possibly one of the most uncomfortable ways

to learn a lesson, either as a child or as an adult. Thankfully, as a professional, I've never found myself in that much of a jam where I didn't leave enough time to produce something that I would be proud to turn into my boss or present to a team of executives. Because even though I turned that book report in that first day back at school in 19-whatever it was, I by no means felt proud of it. I didn't "stand behind" the quality of it, even with my mom's help. Heck, even with John Steinbeck helping me, we simply didn't have the time.

There have also been times throughout my career, like the night at the Preserve, where I found myself pushing it in a sense. Not because I was intentionally procrastinating, but because I didn't realize that a particular task would take as long as I initially thought, or perhaps it was a little more detailed than I believed it to be, once I started to dig through it. So, yes, it's happened and then I needed to hustle, but I can say nothing nearly as egregious as that New Year's Day that, in hindsight, I wish I hadn't looked at as a love-hate relationship. Hindsight is always 20/20, which has been one of the central themes of this book, but what I wouldn't give to be able to have one more of those get togethers, especially with those family members no longer here. Yet another reason to always be grateful for what we have before we no longer have it.

I was a kid, so as I did in the case of the Night Heron

sighting, I will cut myself some slack. As I was typing those words, I pictured myself right back in my YiaYia and Papou's basement, with a big ole plate of goodness, not realizing that those would be the most innocent and easiest days of my life, and that if my biggest worries in the world were doing a measly book report over winter break, well, then not only were those days easy, it meant I had it pretty damn good, too.

Incidentally, my dad's mom, my YiaYia, was the first experience I had dealing with the death of a family member. She died on May 8, 1995, when I was a freshman in high school. The day I visited the  Everglades with my kids last spring, just to jog your memory, was May 7. The following day, I was creating a canvas print of a portrait I took of my kids that day to give to my mom as a Mother's Day present. As I said, we didn't see any birds, but I neglected to share, because I hadn't really thought about it until this point in the book, I did take what I consider to be my favorite picture of my three kids. There is something about the look in their eyes and the youthful innocence along with the rippling water in the background. I knew my mom would love it as much as I did.

As I was processing the photo for printing, it somehow occurred to me right then and there, that was the 25th anniversary of my YiaYia's passing, which I take the time to acknowledge every year. But, when I realized it had been 25, yes, 25 years, I almost had to shake my head in disbelief. In looking back now, it seems she was with me at the very earliest days of my summer journey as well. This is when I normally would throw in something witty to quickly pivot when I felt like things were getting a tad heavy, but let's move on.

Now, there's something to be said about being inspired by the pressure that being on deadline can bring. I was a journalism major in college, was the sports editor of my college newspaper, *The Towerlight*, and interned at the *Baltimore Sun* during those days as well. So, I know sometimes the pressure of writing on deadline almost creates an adrenaline rush that allows us to produce some of our best work. As a quick aside, I also worked at a small family-owned clothing store while in college. So, working in retail, holding an internship at a major metropolitan daily newspaper, serving on the editorial staff of a twice-weekly college newspaper, and taking a full course load of classes was how I spent my last two years in college. Now you might understand even better why being out of work last summer was so hard, beyond the financial aspect.

The point here is that working in those pressure-packed

situations can sometimes bring out our best work. I spent a few years as a freelance sportswriter, working for a few different local papers in Maryland until I moved to Florida, where I covered high school football games on Friday nights (another example of loving to work because this was when I had a full-time career, too). I remember dozens of times when I was covering a high school football game that ended at 9:00 p.m. and have about 90 minutes to run down to the field, double-check my hand-written stats with the official stat keeper, grab a few interviews, run back to the press box—if the high school had one, which it usually didn't, so I'd find the nearest Starbucks with Wi-Fi instead—write my game story, then email it to the editor just in time for a 10:30 p.m. deadline to ensure it would make the following morning's paper.

In my college days, I had the luxury of sitting in and writing, then filing, my story from the comfort of a press box, and the games had official stat keepers, so I didn't have to keep them on my own. But believe it or not, I then had to use dial-up internet and hope the connection was strong enough to be able to email my story to George, the editor of the college sports section of the *Baltimore Sun*, without taking 20 minutes.

The more often I did this, I began to learn more and more tricks of the trade and figured out ways to make life easier for myself, such as having some of the main parts of the article already written before the game was over. Obviously, I had to wait until the game was finished to write the lead, in most cases, but I would write paragraphs throughout the game as big plays occurred, things I knew would most likely make it into the article regardless of the final score. Sometimes I would not even use them, but I had them there just in case. That way, once the game ended, I only had to fill in some of the blanks by adding in the details, such as stats and quotes.

So, giving myself as much time as I possibly could, even though I knew it was tight anyway, is a good example of focusing on juggling a ball as soon as it enters the rotation. In this case, by breaking that ball into different sections, and accomplishing certain aspects of the task right away, and keeping this concept up throughout the game, I didn't have a full game story to write. I had half of one, sometimes less, to simply finish and fine-tune.

No matter how much we may be inspired by the deadline, if you're like me, you'll always go back and find something you feel you could have done better. I will say the experience I had in the press box has made me perform better under pressure in my everyday job, too, because in any profession, in any industry, there will be times when crises occur or something urgent pops, and then it turns into a "drop everything and do this now" situation. So, time will never be on your side, even if it is the only ball you need to focus on at the time, but I can lean upon my experience from my freelance days to help keep me poised and say to myself, "I've done this before. I can do it again."

However, if your boss gives you a week to work on a particular project, whatever it is, don't make the mistake of thinking that's eons of time and then realize—because of all the other balls in the air—that, uh oh, the deadline is tomorrow, and then pull an all-nighter rushing to get it done. It may be passable to turn in, but it likely won't be as high quality as it could have been had you given yourself time to think through the work and do it over the course of the week instead of just one night. Sure, you might get lucky and see a Yellow-crowned Night Heron in five minutes, and your boss may say, "This is the greatest thing I've ever read." But don't count on it.

Conversely, if he gives you a week and you hand it in after two days, thinking you're impressing him by taking initiative and getting it done three days early, think again. He gave you a week for a reason. Most likely for two reasons. One, he probably realizes the request entails more than you may think it does, which happens a lot. And two, he is giving you the courtesy, if not the luxury, to really take that time to be thorough, to think through your work, and then be confident you're handing in something you can feel very proud of in the end.

Because we often have so many balls in the air, we seem to have this knee-jerk reaction to complete tasks quickly so we can then move on to the next. This is understandable, and, frankly, sometimes unavoidable but, when given the time, take it. Because quality oftentimes can only come when we give ourselves the time needed to complete an assignment the right way. Your boss may give it back to you anyway and tell you to try again. And then, the task that should have been over and done with the week before, now starts to interfere with tasks a week later.

The need to get something done seems to be a byproduct of the hectic pace of life as we know it, which is why this time we had during quarantine reminded me that it is indeed okay to slow down. This book is actually a very good example because, as I often find myself doing, I felt the pressure to complete it as quickly as possible because of some self-imposed deadline. Giving yourself a deadline is, of course, good because it helps keep you focused and driven to reach a certain goal, but the deadline must be realistic as well, so you don't end up rushing through something just because you feel you *have* to.

It's then you fail to realize that enjoying the journey and the process of writing the book is as important as actually completing it, and in some ways, more important. I eventually learned this same lesson on my birding journey. Give yourself time to not only produce quality work you feel confident in before the deadline approaches, but the time to enjoy producing the work, too.

Time is the one thing in life we can never get back once its lost. Money, we can. If you've found yourself searching for work and wondering when that money may start flowing again, rest assured, at some point, it will. It always does. The $10,000 in your bank account that was there yesterday will look the exact same tomorrow, too. It always will. But the time we have won't. It never will.

If I could get lost time back, I'd be sitting in YiaYia and Papou's basement on New Year's Day as we speak, getting ready to watch college football without a care in the world. But I can't. Instead, I can learn from the mistakes I made on that one particular New Year's Day and commit to try to never make them again, so time spent with family isn't cut short because I had to work on something that should've been completed days earlier.

Perhaps this lesson turned out to be more profound than I expected it to be when I began to write it, and that's fine with me because it's a lesson we cannot learn often enough, even if we do get lucky and find a Yellow-crowned Night Heron every now and then.

Chapter 6

PUTTING IN MILES: THE CRESTED CARACARA

"Where do Crested Caracaras live anyway?"— Me

The Crested Caracara taken Aug. 4, 2020 in Clewiston, Florida just outside Dinner Island Ranch Nature Preserve.

For those of you who read the preface, and I will forgive you if you didn't, you'll likely recall the gentleman I mentioned by the name of Peter Kaestner. If you didn't read it, I'll save you the trouble of having to retrace your steps. He's the No. 1 birder in the world, according to eBird.com, in terms of how many different species he has observed in his life: 9,261 at the time of me typing this. Kaestner, a Baltimore native, coincidentally, lives in Cockeysville, Maryland, just outside his hometown of Charm City, where I worked while in college in the early 2000s.

How cool that he managed to observe that many different species right there in his home state, and my home state, too, right? Not quite. I'll explain in a moment.

Back in 2009, I took a role with Marriott that had me traveling to Arizona and Texas. Oftentimes I flew out a day early to take advantage of an extra day for sight-seeing, and to experience something locally authentic. I visited both the JFK Museum at Dealey Plaza and the Alamo when in the Lone Star State and places such as the Camelback Mountains in Phoenix. Earlier in my career, I traveled to Boston and did a tour of Fenway Park, and this is true for many other cities, from South Beach to San Francisco.

Had I been a birdwatcher when I was frequenting Texas and Arizona, perhaps I would have added Cedar Ridge Preserve in the Dallas-Fort Worth area or Riparian Preserve at

Water Ranch in Phoenix to the above list. That is exactly what Kaestner did throughout his career working for the U.S. State Department as an American diplomat, literally traveling the globe and thus was able to see birds (and a myriad of the world's most iconic tourist destinations) that he never would have even dreamed of being able to see if he had a "regular 9-to-5 desk job." There is a photo on his Facebook page of him hanging out with the Dali Lama. He will be the first to tell you that he was extraordinarily fortunate to have an opportunity that few will ever have.

Ironically, Kaestner attended Cornell University, home of the world-renowned Ornithology Department but he did not major in Ornithology, despite being a passionate birdwatcher even then. This advice came from a fairly strange source, the dean of the program. An avid birder himself, the professor told a young Peter that if he wanted to still be able to go out and observe and take pictures, he shouldn't necessarily pursue a career in it because he would spend more time in a lab than he would in the field doing what he loved to do.

Kaestner is also known for, and this is incredible, discovering a new species of bird that was previously unknown before he stumbled upon them in 1989 near Bogota, Colombia—the Cundinamarca Antpitta *(Grallaria kaestneri)*. If the "kaestneri" part of the scientific name is making you scratch your head, you guessed it, it was named after him. Think about that for a second. Imagine you're out and about one day, taking part in your favorite hobby and then discover something that no one else before you ever had. It would be like looking up at the sky one night, gazing at the stars, only to quickly realize that the big bright one you've been marveling at for the last 10 minutes was not a star but actually an undiscovered planet. And then they named it *Planet Bob Smith* (if, of course, your name was Bob Smith).

Now, I am not suggesting that to be successful in this hobby or in any hobby, or to be successful in your job, you need to choose a career that takes you around the world. However, sometimes you do have to put in the miles to experience things that staying put in one place simply won't allow. And, as I'll touch on later, sometimes you may have to move to find the next great opportunity but more on that in a second. First, my own birding story that inspired this chapter.

While I had found a fair amount of success observing a wide variety of species within the tri-county area (Broward, Palm Beach, and Miami-Dade) a couple months into birding, as I continued to leaf through my *Birds of Florida* book, I quickly discovered if I wanted to see certain species, I'd need to venture out just a little bit. It would be easy to assume, as I did early on in my birding endeavors, that if a bird is common in say

Okeechobee County (only a couple counties away), it would also be fairly common in Broward. Why not, right? This, of course, is not the case. In fact, even birds that are common in certain parts of Broward County may not be found in other parts that are 20 minutes away. But when I saw images of the Crested Caracara in my book, I knew I had to see one for myself.

The Crested Caracara is a threatened species in Florida due to habitat loss. It can be found further inland and north of Broward. Since I am a fan of "instant gratification," I knew I needed to make it happen soon after reading about it. As in, if I read about a Crested Caracara on a Friday, I'd basically be making plans in my own head, to try and see one on Saturday. It wasn't exactly the next day when we'd venture out, but close.

I have always been this way and it's because—as the saying goes—life is short, and you never know when you'll have another chance. If these last several months have taught us anything, it's exactly that. Take advantage of the time you have and seize the opportunities to experience something new while you have the chance, because that chance may not be there tomorrow.

When I lived in the Washington, D.C., area, I always tried to take advantage of significant historical events taking place nearby, such as presidential inaugurations, regardless of who was taking office, simply because it was a rare opportunity that I was fortunate to be able to witness as a "local."

In the spring of 2013, I had the urge to see the Cherry Blossoms for the first time. Sometimes we get caught in the daily grind so much, we take for granted our ability to see something other people in the country would be envious of. Seeing the Cherry Blossoms at the tidal basin every spring against the backdrop of the Jefferson Memorial and Washington Monument, would fall into this category. But, for one reason or another, I never made time for it. So, on a whim, I took the rare day off work during "peak bloom" and the family and I went. And to this day, I am still glad I did because, and I had no idea at the time, by the fall of that same year, I would no longer be living in the area, and, thus, haven't had the chance since then to experience this beautiful annual event so easily.

So, in early August, I began to research best spots to see a Crested Caracara and identified a couple of sites, both of which were about 90 minutes away—one in Hendry County and the other in Collier County.

The thing about birds, or any wildlife, is there is obviously no guarantee that you'll actually see what you head out to look for on a particular day. It isn't like going sight-seeing in Washington, D.C., and arriving at the Jefferson Memorial only to discover it isn't there. Of course, it will be there but with wildlife, birds notably, it truly can sometimes come down to luck. But, regardless, if I even had a chance to see one, I knew the only way to do so was to put in the miles and venture outside my own area and take a bit of a chance, knowing that nothing was guaranteed.

On Tuesday, August 4, we set out for Dinner Island Ranch Nature Preserve in Clewiston (Hendry County) with one goal in mind and thus *Mission: Find the Crested Caracara* was underway. The boys and I hopped in the car, again, with snacks and bug-spray in tow. Emma got out of "Field Trip Day" when she received a better offer—a playdate with her best friend a few doors down. Who can blame her?

While we were going to a specific location, the other thing I had heard about this particular bird is that it can also be found on the sides of roads within the vicinity of the park itself, either up in a tree or perched on a stump. So, as we neared the area, I told the boys to keep their eyes open so we could cover all sides—me looking ahead, Dylan looking right, and Noah looking left.

We didn't see one on the drive there, but I wasn't really expecting to. We pulled into Dinner Island and it was massive, but my boys were delighted to discover, unlike most of the places we had been to already that summer, this place is predominantly a drive-through refuge. There were not a ton of opportunities to get out and walk around, so you can do most of your observations from the comfort of your air-conditioned car. And, based on how the driving paths were laid out, the view from the car was just as good as it would be if you got out and walked. The bug-spray was given the day off.

There is always something special about visiting a new park or preserve, something about being in "uncharted territory" for the first time. Just like the first time you watched your favorite movie. Even if you

Black-Bellied Whistling Ducks. Aug. 2020. Clewiston, Fla.

enjoy watching it repeatedly (*Back to the Future* anyone?) there is nothing like the first time you see it. As we drove around, we saw several different species, including some new ones for me: Glossy Ibis, closely related to the much more ubiquitous White Ibis, which I have seen thousands of in my life.

Seriously, I once saw what must've been 400 in a grouping of pine trees one day. But the Glossy Ibis is not nearly as common. A pair of Black-Bellied Whistling Ducks was another new species for me. And while both of those new observations were cool, don't get me wrong, they weren't enough. After all, we were not on *Mission: Find the Glossy Ibis and Black-Bellied Whistling Duck.*

This, by the way, is another lesson. When you set out on

an expedition such as this, with a specific species in mind, you do run the risk of leaving disappointed. As mentioned, there is no guarantee of seeing what you set out to see, even if you think positive thoughts. The importance of thinking positively is without question one of the top learnings from these past few months. Even that is not failproof, but the lesson here is this: while it is okay to allow yourself to be disappointed for not obtaining a goal—in this case, seeing a specific bird you drove a relatively lengthy distance to see—you shouldn't let that disappointment supersede any joy you experience while attempting to achieve your goal.

For example, Dylan's baseball team reached the championship in his youth baseball league in 2018 and lost. It was very disappointing, but he also needed to keep in mind, as I encouraged him to do at the time, that the team had lots of reason to celebrate. Even reaching the championship in and of itself was an accomplishment. So, again, yes, it's fine to be a little down if you don't get the result you hoped for but also remember to find joy in the other "wins" you had while trying. In my case, two new birds. In Dylan's case, winning the division title that enabled the team to get to the league championship. I, of course, should note, in 2019, one year later, his team did in fact win the entire thing.

Back to Dinner Island Ranch. About 45 minutes in, there

were still no sightings of the Crested Caracara, but as I just shared in the previous chapter, putting in time is another key component of achieving success. So, I was determined to keep trying a little longer. A half-hour is hardly any time at all in the big scheme of things, so I wasn't giving up hope. Not yet anyway. Seeing one was still a possibility.

Until I looked at the clock, realized it was almost 2:00 p.m. and the boys hadn't eaten lunch yet. Oops. Knowing a Snickers bar and some corn chips would not be a suitable answer to "What did the boys eat for lunch?" and fearful I would be removed from my role as Camp Counselor Dad by the Head Counselor, who was still back home working, I decided to call it and head out to get the boys something that contained some nutritional content. Again, not discouraged yet because if you recall, I said there were two places I had in mind. So, after lunch, we'd head there next, which was in Immokalee in Collier County.

In fact, this was the more likely of the two places I'd be able to see one based on my research. I chose the other one first because I knew it provided the opportunity to see a broader array of species, and that proved to be true, thanks to my Glossy Ibis and the Whistling Ducks, neither of which I would see at the Caracara Preserve in Immokalee. Yes, there is actually a preserve named after this bird based on the fact that they "nest and forage within the preserve and surrounding agricultural and conservation lands," according to the preserve's website. And don't ask why I didn't just start there if I am all about instant gratification. I am also about keeping hope alive and suspending disbelief until the absolute last possible minute, too.

We pulled out of Dinner Island Ranch and headed toward Subway about 15 minutes away and as I was driving west on Rt. 29, for some reason, I looked up and to the left at a tall tree I was approaching (while keeping my eyes also on the road—it was a clear stretch with no other cars nearby). I've noticed that I do this quite often now. After seeing a family of Red-shouldered Hawks hanging out on a series of lamp posts one day, I've learned you never know when you'll pass a cool bird and a great photo opportunity. As I got closer, what caught my attention began to come into focus. Could it be? As I passed under the tree, my head swiveled to the left and it was confirmed: yes, indeed! A Crested Caracara. But I had passed it. So, I made a U-Turn as soon as I could, quietly praying that he'd still be there.

With larger birds of prey, such as Hawks, Ospreys, and Eagles, it was a safe bet they would be. They tend to perch for a while as they survey the area and don't ever appear to be in much of a hurry. If it were a small songbird that tends to flutter around at an almost spastic pace, not a chance. So, I was fairly confident the Caracara would still be there, too.

Within seconds, I was headed back in the other direction

and as I got closer, I could already tell he was still there. Score. Now, the question was: would he stay there once I stopped and tried to grab a picture? That is also a consideration. A big one, in fact. As I had experienced several times already, a Red-Shouldered Hawk could sit in the same spot quite contently for 20 minutes, and he'd be just as content with me standing right along with him. Bui as soon as I start to reach for the camera, he would fly away as if it's his job. I almost wonder if they do this to mess with me. Maybe partially so. It could also be that they are scared. I don't know though because I haven't yet had a chance to ask one.

Because of his size and because of my vantage point, I did not need to get out of my car. The bug-spray continues to get a free pass. I lowered the passenger side window, unbuckled my seat belt (yes, I wear one and that detail is for you, mom), leaned over, zoomed in, and clicked away. I had a great view and felt confident I was able to do this incredible species justice with the photos I had taken, as much as a photo can anyway. I was able to preview the shots right then and there on the camera and could tell they'd turn out great. But, for good measure, I took about a dozen more because, why not? This of course is a benefit of no longer having to use film. While there is technically a limit to what a memory card will hold, you never truly have to worry about "running out of film."

All in, I took about 20 or so shots. Mission accomplished. We headed to lunch and I drove there like I was Tom Brady. Maybe I should have said Tom Cruise to keep with the "Mission" theme, but to be honest, I felt more like a seven-time Super Bowl Champion than I did anything else. And, the boys were excited, too. Maybe it's that they were excited *for* me. Maybe they get joy by seeing me get joy. As parents, we are happy when our children are happy, and we are sad when they are sad. Perhaps our children are more emotionally in-tune than we give them credit for, and they mirror our emotions just as we do. Regardless, they too were on Cloud Nine as we continued down the road. On second thought, maybe their joy was because they knew lunch was next. I only tease. I knew they were happy, and it was not lost on me then, nor is it now, that "I am happy for dad" was probably the main reason why. I love those kids.

Oh, and since I mentioned that after Subway, we planned to head to the Caracara Preserve, you might be wondering if we still did, even though we already completed our "Mission." The  answer is, yes. And we saw another one. And just like the first sighting, not within the preserve itself, but hanging out on a tree just outside it. Right next to a Red-shouldered Hawk.

There is one other thing you should know about that day's outing and if you think I am throwing this in for dramatic effect, I will gladly show you my cell phone records (see, I told you this would happen a couple times). On the way home, and still feeling like Tom Brady, I received a phone call from a recruiter from a company I had been interviewing with all summer. And yes, I mean *all* summer. I began the interview process June 9, the day before my fortieth birthday. I went through six rounds. Six. As she delivered the news that the company had decided to move forward with another candidate, I fought back the tears as I told her I understood the decision, which, truth be told, I didn't. My two boys were watching, which is why I felt the need to hide my emotions.

Now, I want to clarify two things. First, the tears were not because of the rejection directly. In my 17 years in the corporate world, I had applied for jobs before and, despite my confidence that I was qualified, I did not end up getting some of them. It happens. To most of us, if not all of us. So, no, I do not usually get emotional, let alone have to hold back tears when I don't land a job. In this case, though, it wasn't about *this* job. On top of that, it also wasn't about *me*, either. Meaning, I was not feeling sorry for myself or sad for myself.

As I have shared many times before, despite being out of work for the first time in my career, I considered myself extremely fortunate in a number of ways. And I still do.

So, the tears were not about me, the job, or my own personal circumstance. It was the thought that I was somehow letting my family down. My boys, who again, were five feet away from me, and who I have had countless conversations with over the years about how they can grow up to be anything they want. And here I was, feeling as though I was somehow a failure, and to some degree, a fraud.

I stayed positive 99 percent of the time I was looking for work but occasionally, I let feelings of self-defeat and doubt creep in, and in moments such as hearing those recruiter's words echoing in my head, almost in slow motion, well, sometimes there just simply isn't any comfort to be found.

Secondly, showing emotion is nothing to be ashamed of either, but I felt like I needed to be strong for them. I had done my best throughout those trying months to not give them any reason to worry. About money. About my psyche. Or about me in general. Our kids shouldn't have to worry about us. They are kids but as I said they feel our happiness, they feel our sadness, too. As the call ended, the three of us sat there quietly as if none of us wanted to acknowledge what had just happened. They didn't ask me but, as I sat there behind a pair of dark sunglasses, without me saying anything, they both knew what the phone call was. And they both knew how it made me feel and both let out, around the same time, a simple "I'm sorry dad. It'll be okay." Like I said, I love those kids.

It was tough news to hear as I continued to wonder just when that next opportunity would come my way. Not just because I had made it so far, only to have it snatched away after a 30-second phone call, but because I had invested two months of my time and an incredible amount of energy and passion into each round of the interview process. But, like I said with birding, nothing is guaranteed.

As we continued the drive, I wasn't exactly feeling like Tom Brady, but I was okay. After all, I had just seen not one, but two, Crested Caracaras, as well as some Glossy Ibises and the Black-Bellied Whistling Ducks. When I say that the birds saved me last summer, perhaps now you know exactly what I mean.

By the time we got home, since the phone call came when we were still about an hour out, I already had a chance to calm myself down and in the spirit of keeping up the positive thinking, realized that this was just a sign this particular job was not for me. And it meant I was one step closer to the one that was. The opportunity to have those thoughts while driving, is yet another benefit of venturing out a bit.

Incidentally, it is that type of phone call where my philosophy of "keeping hope alive" until the last possible minute comes from. Even though I felt confident I had done well in the final round of the process, I began to doubt that I would receive an offer. I just had a hunch that a call of that nature was coming but, again, in the spirit of keeping that hope alive, I essentially told myself until I hear otherwise, just assume you will get the job. That phone call, looking back now in hindsight, was a relief. At least I knew it was a "no," and I could move on. Because, as yet another Tom—Tom Petty—once reminded us, "The waiting is the hardest part." (I bet you read that while singing it, didn't you? Don't lie).

Now, before I share the takeaways from this chapter and discuss how these lessons can apply to one's personal and professional endeavors, I should mention, Kaestner is still at it. I've kept up with his adventures via his Facebook page where he publicly shares his journeys. In August, he flew to Phoenix for the second time that summer in search of an Eared Quetzal, one of only a relatively small number of birds that eluded his "lifer list." He was unsuccessful his first time but, in August, like mine was, *Mission: Eared Quetzal* was a success. Imagine flying home from Arizona to Maryland after not seeing one. If I felt like Tom Brady after my successful Crested Caracara outing, Kaestner must've felt like the Buffalo Bills of the 1990s after losing four consecutive Super Bowls but as I told Dylan, even getting there is cause for celebration. Just ask Jim Kelley.

While there were a few lessons peppered into this chapter, the main takeaway is all about the importance of stepping outside of your own backyard. To branch out. To experience something new. Something unfamiliar. And that can only happen when you have the courage to leave the nest. (No pun intended. Okay, it was intended).

I mentioned earlier, you don't have to travel around the globe, or even move, to achieve personal or professional success. I know many people who haven't moved and certainly live fulfilling, successful lives. However, at the same time, there will be moments in your life where you may find yourself faced with a choice to stay close to home, or "put in the miles" and take a chance.

As I alluded to earlier in this chapter, this was exactly what happened to me in September of 2013. I had grown up in Montgomery County, Maryland, in the suburbs of Washington, D.C., and so did Kristie. I loved living there and growing up there. I loved the idea of raising my children there, too. I never envisioned leaving, nor had I ever really planned to. Why would I? It provided everything anyone would ever need—nice neighborhoods with top-notch schools, an incredibly rich and diverse culture with countless museums and historical sites, great professional sports franchises that I spent my life devoted to, and weather that allows you to experience the four seasons with ski resorts, mountains, parks, and beaches all within a reasonable drive. Not to mention, I still had lots of family there as well as friends, and, of course, a career I loved.

But again, sometimes in life you are faced with opportunities that may never come your way again. It was a typical fall Sunday, though technically still summer, and I was in my post-summer blues state as we had just returned home from our last beach vacation of the year. It was a mini getaway with my dad, who had rented a large house right on the sand. I was sitting on the couch, and I remember the exact date and what I was doing—September 15, 2013, and I was watching football, just fiddling with my phone.

I opened LinkedIn and, like when I spotted the Crested Caracara, my eyes were immediately drawn to the red "1" on the top of the screen, which indicated I had one new message in my inbox. It was from a recruiter at Miami-based Carnival Cruise Line that would ultimately, without being hyperbolic, change my life in unimaginable ways. Vanessa was reaching out to see if I would be interested in posting for and interviewing for a newly created position to lead employee communications at "the World's Most Popular Cruise Line."

I showed it to Kristie. She quickly joked back, "Do not tell your mom!" Let me explain. My mom had moved to Miami just three months before, after Rick accepted a job offer down here himself, and, subsequently, she did as well. As soon as she moved to Florida, the questions started to come in about when Kristie and I were moving to Florida. "Never," I quipped back. I should mention that, as much as my mother loves me, I am not blind to the fact this was predominately about two people in particular: my two sons, Dylan and Noah. (Emma was not yet born. She is the only native Floridian among us).

So, when the message came in from Carnival, Kristie advised me not to tell my mom simply because she didn't want me to get my mother's hopes up too soon because at that point, I had no idea how legitimate the offer was. Not that I questioned Vanessa's intentions, it's just that when you receive a message like that, you never know if you are one of 100 people to receive it, one of 10, or one of one. I still don't know the answer to that question, but I do know I was the one who got the job!

After my initial reply expressing interest, the next three weeks were somewhat of a whirlwind. Later that same week I had a video conference with my would-be manager, and on October 1, two weeks after the initial LinkedIn message, I was on a plane to Miami to meet with seven or eight people the following day, including the CFO of the company. I had dinner with my mom and Rick, too, the night I arrived because, at that point, I obviously had to let them know, and I also appreciated their perspective and advice as I prepared for the marathon day of interviews.

As I was leaving town on October 2, and was walking through security at the airport, my phone rang, and Carnival officially offered me the job. To say that flight home was somewhat surreal would be putting it mildly. My mind raced the entire flight, and the Tanqueray and tonic didn't do much to change that, but it didn't stop me from ordering a second one just to be sure.

Kristie and I, as any couple would do, spent the next few days weighing every pro and con imaginable. Carnival was generous in that they gave me ample time to make the decision, but I knew I'd have to make one soon. At the end of the day, I'll be honest, that pro-con list was basically split right down the middle. So, we both looked at each other and said, why not? I don't say this to sound flip. We, as I said, did our due diligence and with the somewhat limited time we had, did our best to research cities, schools, neighborhoods, housing prices, beaches, etc., etc. But, when all is said and done, when you are faced with such a decision and the good and the bad are pretty much neck and neck, ultimately it will often come down to a "gut decision."

One important note to add. My mother-in-law, Linda, died of breast cancer in 2007, a little more than three years after Kristie and I were married. In fact, the day we returned from our honeymoon, was the day we learned of her diagnosis. Kristie losing her mother when she was 28 was obviously a life-changing event for her (and me, too). Linda was as sweet a soul as there ever was, and my coffee buddy. In fact, we spent many hours at Borders Books in Gaithersburg, Maryland, browsing through books and chatting about life, and sipping on coffee—at least I did. I used to tease her that she only ordered it to look cool because we'd leave, and her mug would be full. But, Linda, if there's a bookstore up there, this one is for you.

It was around this time, too, that the idea of one day leaving Maryland for a new adventure first occurred to us. But, again, one of those things that we talk about, but never pursue. Until that email showed up in m inbox. It's a decision we made and once we did, never looked back. Sure, there are moments when I miss Maryland, mostly family and friends who still live there. My father and stepmom, Wendy, notably, plus numerous cousins and childhood friends, but they are as much a part of my life now as they ever have been. And, yet another lesson from this is, sometimes to gain or experience something new, it requires you to give up something in return. Life can sometimes be a series of trade-offs and you just hope the choices you make along the way yield more gains than losses. If you can say that, then you've done well.

Oh, and the Cherry Blossoms too. I also miss the Cherry Blossoms, but at least I got to see them once.

Before I get any further, allow me to share another one of those too-good-to-be-true moments. After I published the blog on the Northern Cardinal, my friend Vanessa (yes that

Vanessa—we keep in touch) sent me a text to let me know she enjoyed reading the blog, then shared that near her house was a Bald Eagle's nest. This is fitting for this chapter for two reasons. One, it was Vanessa—the person who played arguably the largest role in the fact I am now living in Florida—who shared this information with me. Two, this is also another classic example of my need for instant gratification. Because she did so on Thursday, May 21. I went and saw the Bald Eagles the next day, Friday, May 22. And, like I said, just in time for Memorial Day Weekend.

Moving states is not the only way to achieve this concept of stepping out of your comfort zone. It also doesn't mean you need to pursue a career like Kaestner either. As much as he loved his job, as I have read about him quite a bit, I also know that he, too, had to make some trade-offs that weren't always easy. The point is you will ultimately need to decide how important it is to you to be able to experience what the world has to offer. You cannot see the Eiffel Tower if you don't ever want to visit Paris. In any case, there are numerous ways to achieve this concept whether personally or professionally, and here are three examples.

My good childhood friend, Nick, whom I have known since kindergarten, on multiple occasions, took long-term assignments through his company that allowed him to live in New York City as well as London. Nick, of all people, can tell you just what might happen when you step outside your comfort zone. He met his wife, Carly, on a return flight from London. (As I understand it, calling a female friend a "bird" is popular British slang. Thus, if I thought a Crested Caracara was worth putting in miles for, it's safe to assume that Nick's "bird" was a much more significant example of this).

My older brother, John, is a college football coach, and while it can be a stressful profession, there are a number of perks. Since his oldest daughter was born, he has held roles in Nebraska, North Carolina, Maryland, and, as of last season, Florida State (go Noles). Before he and his wife, Billie, had kids they also lived in Kansas (where they met) and Louisiana. For John and Billie, that's six states to experience and, for their four oldest kids, Addy, Johnny, Sophia, and Rylee, they've lived in the four I mentioned above. Young Jack, born in 2019, has only lived in two. What a slacker.

While it of course has its inherent challenges, as a mom, Billie shares that being able to expose her kids to different parts of the country is one of the biggest benefits of being part of the college football coaching community.

"One of the blessings of moving around so much is being able to explore new cities all over the country," she said. "It's really helped us as a family become adaptable, flexible, and has enabled us to experience new places we wouldn't ordinarily be able to otherwise."

Two other childhood friends of mine, Greg and Jennifer, made the decision to live in Como, Italy, (yes, that is also where George Clooney spends a lot of time in case it sounds familiar) for about 18 months when their first, and, at the time, only daughter, Julia, was about two years old in what Greg referred to as "pretirement." I don't know if he invented that term, but I'll give him credit anyway. His belief is that oftentimes, you're in better shape and can get more out of this time when you're younger than you may be able to when you're older and at true retirement age.

"The experience was like no other. As a new father, I got to connect with my wife and daughter on a deep and profound level that few ever experience," Greg recalls, looking back seven years later. "We were able to enrich our lives with a new cultural awaking that is still in our core today. And, frankly, we got to see some of the coolest sh*t of our lives!"

Greg and Jen's decision, by the way, as I have shared with him on multiple occasions, is partially what inspired me to make the move to Florida. It helped reinforce what I have known and believed all along, which again, is that life is short, and we must seize the opportunities before us while we can.

That concept also reminds me of the Helen Keller quote, which I adopted as my mantra throughout the move to Florida, which is, "Life is either a daring adventure or nothing at all."

How poignant. And that's how we had to approach it. From an initial email on September 15 to living in Florida by November 1. When I think back, I almost shake my head with how we pulled that off without many hiccups, if any at all. So, yes, the poignant words of Helen Keller were there to remind us that we just needed to view everything that came our way, good or bad, as simply part of the adventure.

Just as poignant as Keller's are the wise words of Ferris Bueller, "Life moves pretty fast. If you don't stop and look around once in a while, you may miss it."

Don't miss it, folks. Put in the miles and go look for it today. Not tomorrow. If you wait, you might miss it. After all, not everything is as patient as a Crested Caracara. It may fly away.

Chapter 7

PREPAREDNESS AND PREPARATION: RED-HEADED WOODPECKER

"Dad, what does a Red-headed Woodpecker sound like?"
— My Son, Dylan

The Florida Scrub-Jay taken August 2020 at Jon Dickinson State Park, Martin County, Florida.

First, in case you're curious, no, that is not a Red-headed Woodpecker on the previous page. Yes, I have used the birds that inspire the chapter titles in each of the title pages thus far but, no, that is not a Red-headed Woodpecker, and you'll find out why later. First, I'll share a story from earlier in my career.

There was a person I once worked with that used to seem to derive pleasure in making people squirm in their seats if they came to a meeting without having done the proper amount of preparation first. I am not even going to tell you whether this person was male or female, or how long ago it was, because I don't want anyone that I've previously worked with trying to guess who I am talking about (though I bet they can regardless).

This person would actually be flattered, now that I think about it, to realize they had such a reputation, and to some degree they should be, because they were, after all, teaching these under-prepared professionals, usually those who were more junior in the organization, a valuable lesson that was beneficial to learn early in their careers. The fact that this person seemed to enjoy going for the jugular, even after the point was made, is what made it seem uncomfortable for others in the room.

To me, once they asked a question that proved the employee should probably go back and do some more research first, the presentation should have ended, and we should've moved to the next topic on the agenda. This person would ask questions over and over, knowing the presenter did not know the answer before they even asked it.

"Did you run this by 'so and so' first for feedback?" No, I did not.

"Did you confirm the timing works based on all other priorities and initiatives happening at the same time?" No, I did not.

"Did you factor in 'XYZ' when you came up with 'ZYX'?" No, I did not.

This would go on for several more minutes, with a series of "No, I did not" and "I don't know" or "I hadn't thought about that" type answers playing on repeat for what felt like an eternity for the presenter, I'm sure, but I suppose that it helped make the lesson more impactful, because if I felt uncomfortable as an observer, I can only imagine how the subjects of this person's inquisition felt. Perhaps they were made so uncomfortable to the point where they'd never dare come to a meeting to share a proposal or present on a topic without having done their "homework" first. Once was enough.

Once was enough for me when I took a drive to a place, while only one county away—Palm Beach County, which I had been to dozens of times over the last few months—it was toward the northwest end of the county, and, thus, still an hour or so away. Normally an hour is not a big deal. I had been to several places that far away, if not more, but this was a little different. As shared in earlier chapters, the Crested Caracara being the best example, there have been other occasions where I would drive to a place looking for a specific species. There is always risk in this, as I knew, but at least in the Caracara example, I also knew that even if I didn't see one, I'd still see plenty of other new birds and it turned out to be true. This time though, I was going to a park where being able to see anything else was also slim. It was an "all or nothing" proposition.

Here's the set-up. On the previous Saturday, I took a drive solo—which was a rarity on a weekend—to a place even further away, close to 90 minutes in Jupiter on the lookout for the only bird that is 100 percent confined to the state of Florida: The Florida Scrub-Jay, which many believe should be the official state bird of Florida but, as I would discover through research, they could not be found in Broward County.

After doing some "homework," I learned that the closest place they could be commonly seen is in Martin County, in Jupiter, just a couple miles over the Palm Beach County line. I'd been to Jupiter a few times since moving to Florida, each time to dine at The Woods, the upscale sports bar and restaurant owned by Tiger Woods himself. Just like the state of Florida is the only place to find the Florida Scrub-Jay, similarly, Jupiter is the only place in the country where you can visit the restaurant personally owned by the greatest golfer in history.

Once I knew Martin County was my best option, I then

went a step further to seek the advice of people on Facebook about which park provided the best chance. It turns out that Jon Dickinson State Park is not only where they can be most commonly found, it's pretty much guaranteed you'll see one whenever you went. I've stated before there is never a guarantee when looking to photograph wildlife, but this is as close as it gets to a sure thing because the park is known for essentially being the official habitat of the Florida Scrub-Jay. Like many of the parks I have visited, though, Dickinson Park is massive, and so after the many comments came in suggesting it, and after looking the park up online myself, I asked if anyone had any specific tips as to where within the park I could best find them.

I was then given step-by-step guidance, including turn-by-turn directions on where to park and where to head once I got out of my car, by a very helpful gentleman named Paul (yet another teaser for my chapter on peers). He then casually dropped, "You can also find Red-headed Woodpeckers there, too." In hindsight, I wish he hadn't said it. More on that in a minute.

I arrived at the park right as it opened, which would allow me to get home by noon after a (hopefully) successful expedition to see the Florida

Scrub-Jay. Thanks to the information I was provided, along with the research I had done on my own, I found one within the first five minutes. I took dozens of pictures while there and saw about seven or eight of them in total.

The trip was a total success, but, then my mind quickly shifted to, "oh yeah—the Red Heads!" When Paul mentioned the possibility of me seeing one there—another species not found in Broward due to their specific habitat needs—he also mentioned that it would also be not as much of a lock as seeing the Scrub-Jay would be. So, I looked around some more, saw some more Scrub-Jays, among other things, but no Red-headed Woodpecker. The persistence and perseverance in me wanted to keep looking (another carryover lesson), but I also knew I needed to head out soon. Because, after all, the Florida Scrub-Jay, which was my original "target," was successfully seen and photographed and that should have been enough for me to feel very happy about that morning's outing. And it was. Gratitude for what we have, not feeling bad for what we don't—another lesson learned on the birding trail.

I headed home content, truly, and uploaded then shared my Scrub-Jay photos later that day. Paul congratulated me on the great pictures, I thanked him for his helpful guidance, and mentioned that I would have to go back at some point because the Red-headed Woodpeckers were not to be found that day.

That brings me back to the trip the following Friday afternoon, six days later (remember my penchant for instant gratification?) when the boys and I headed to the north end of Palm Beach County. Emma, once again, had a better offer—this time, a sleepover with Grammy (my mom). Again, who could blame her? So, when I mentioned to Paul the week before that it, "Looks like I'll be headed back to Jupiter again soon!" he sent me a message saying they can also be found somewhere a little closer, at a park called Okecholee South, which is mostly known for its equestrian arena, where equestrians and horseback riders can leverage the park's amenities for training and in a non-COVID world, competing. Cool, but it's not known for birds. At all. But he told me he had seen them there many times and it was a little closer and because of my unsuccessful attempt the week before, I thought, why not try a new spot even if it was only just *slightly* closer?

The boys and I went there that day, but this time, I didn't have the same success as I did when Paul gave me the step-by-step guidance on the Scrub-Jay. Because, well, this time I didn't have that level of detail. Let me clarify, I am not suggesting he needed to proactively provide it. At all. I didn't ask him, nor did I do any "homework" of my own to increase my chances either. So, I made a rookie mistake even though this was several months in at this point. Perhaps, going back to my lesson on "Egrets before

Ovenbirds," subconsciously I didn't think I needed any more guidance and knew what I was doing.

When we arrived at the park, not surprisingly, it was as big as most of the other places we'd been to. I didn't know where to begin. I'll spare the details (such as Noah somehow losing his eyeglasses at some point along the way—that was a fun one to try to explain later that night), but we drove from area to area, within the park, stumbled around for a few minutes, got back in the car, and tried again. This went on for about an hour or so until I finally decided to message Paul to see if he had any more details to provide. He graciously did.

"Park by the boat ramp and look at the pine snags on the right side of the parking lot." A pine snag, by the way, is a dead pine tree basically and that's where they live. There are not nearly enough of them in Broward, due to development, for them to live here. We have plenty of other Woodpecker species here— Downy, Red-headed Woodpecker, and Pileated for example—all of which I've seen and photographed these last few months. I should also note the boat ramp parking lot is the first one on your left when you arrive. Of course. More "shoulda done more homework, Matt" for the stack.

The best lesson of all though, came courtesy of my older son, Dylan, when he said, after we were in the boat ramp area at the spot, "Dad, what does a Red-headed Woodpecker sound like?" Suddenly, I felt like one of those unsuspecting presenters at my old company, sharing a PowerPoint with only half-baked ideas. "Umm, good question, Dylan. I don't know."

Now, thanks to technology, I was able to pull up his call right away. But the fact I didn't do this ahead of time meant we may have heard one already. We were there for more than an hour at that point. It also meant I could have heard one the week before when I was out and about looking for Scrub-Jays, too. Often, you'll hear a bird before you see it. But once you do, you can key in on an area and search for other clues for its location.

We headed home, unsuccessful, with a lost pair of glasses to boot, as well as being hot and tired. I have said before, sometimes just being outdoors, immersing yourself in the pursuit is reward enough. Not this time.

I was once attending a college football game at the University of Nebraska when my brother, John, was coaching there. It. Was. Freezing. But they won. Barely. (31-17. I had to look that up, truth be told, but if you wonder why I'd call that "barely," it's because Nebraska scored 18 points in the final quarter, so it was touch and go). I joked to my father after the game, I'd have been real ticked off if they lost. Sitting in the bitter cold for four hours is more than worth it when the team you're supporting wins, especially one where your older brother is coaching. Sitting in that same bitter cold when they lose, just plain stinks, even *if* your older brother is out there coaching.

So, no, this was not the most fun car ride home for us that day.

But I did learn a valuable lesson on the importance of preparation, and for that, I guess you could say it was worth it after all. I should note that I still haven't found a Red-headed Woodpecker but earlier lessons on patience remind me that I will eventually.

And now you know why the Florida Scrub-Jay is the bird used to illustrate the title page of this chapter. Because even though the Red-headed Woodpecker taught me a tough lesson on the lack of preparation, the Scrub-Jay is a satisfying reminder of the payoff when you do take the time to prepare. Plus, I don't have a photo of a Red-headed Woodpecker, remember? Don't rub it in.

Having spent a significant amount of time these last six months in "homeschool dad" mode, certainly the lesson on preparation is another one we work hard, every day, to instill in our kids, and yet another one we don't always keep top of mind as adults. We spend countless hours trying to teach good study habits we hope serve them well throughout their life, even after they, to borrow the phrase again, "leave the nest."

"Did you write down your homework?" No, I'll remember. "Good for you, write it down anyway so you can feel proud of yourself for proving me wrong when I use your written-down version to cross-reference when I check your homework later."

I am sure that I had to learn the hard way about preparation when I was a kid, too, that's for sure. Now that I give it some thought, I seem to recall a spelling test I didn't even know I had and got every question wrong because it was double-L words, and I didn't know a single one. Not one. 0/25. Yes, really. Or should I say, realy. Because that was one of them. Why do I remember this? Well, because it was painful as heck to learn an important lesson that way when I was about nine years old. I wish I could say I learned it well enough to never make that mistake again, but it's doubtful. I am sure I had a few hiccups after that.

From a career standpoint, I can say that I can't remember anything too horrifying, and, believe me, I'd tell you. I am an open book as I write this. I am sure I had a few but maybe they were never that severe because I had enough of them in my youth to last a lifetime, but I do recall a time early in my career when I went into my boss's office and told him about a "problem" I had discovered with a project I was leading. He asked me what my thoughts were for a solution. I didn't have one, so he told me to come back when I did. I cannot recall the specifics of the project, but that's unimportant because it did teach me the lesson on thinking through various potential outcomes.

This is a good example of preparation but, also, a lesson on resourcefulness, too, because it forced me to be creative and problem-solve. I haven't been to a boss's office since without having a "but here's what I'm thinking we do…" after calling his or her attention to a potential roadblock.

Preparation comes in handy in all aspects of life, even ones you may not assume would warrant needing a ton of homework. It's no secret to anyone who knows me, even casually, that I am huge Disney fan, which I've mentioned at various points in this book. However, none of you reading this—other than those who knew me already—are aware of just how big of a fan I am. When I admitted in the opening passages of this book that I hadn't reached "expert-level" birder status to write a book about birding exclusively and instead chose to write one on the lessons it provided that I wanted to share with others, I can say with a high level of confidence that I *could* write one about Disney. Walt Disney World Resort in Orlando, to be more specific. So could a lot of other people, too, people with a much larger social media following than me because the Disney social media "influencer" and blogger community is as massive as Dickinson Park.

As a matter of fact, earlier in this book I mentioned that prior to Mother's Day on May 10, that the last time I saw my mom and Rick was on March 7, the day of Dylan's opening day baseball game (and his last one too). I didn't mention though that later that same day we headed to the Most Magical Place on Earth for a little one-night getaway, mainly to check out the new Mickey and Minnie's Runaway Railway attraction at Disney's Hollywood Studios which had opened earlier that same week, as well as the opening weekend of Epcot's International Flower and Garden Festival, no doubt my favorite time of year to visit that park. Flower and Garden? Maybe I've always been a nature enthusiast at heart after all.

In looking back, this was the last "normal" weekend before the COVID pandemic hit hard, as that following Friday ushered in the start of quarantine. By the following Monday, Disney World closed for the first time since Hurricane Maria in 2017 and the first time it ever shut down for longer than just a handful of days.

Anyway, given that I am the resident Disney expert among my friends, I have probably received 50 messages since moving to Florida from folks asking for my advice on how they can make the most of their Disney vacation. I am always flattered. Sometimes I'll receive one like, "I'll be in Orlando for a few days and we have one day for Disney and want to do Magic Kingdom. What do I need to do?"

The first piece of advice I give anyone, whether going for a week or a day, is this…drum roll, please: "Just relax and have fun and realize that no matter what you do, you'll have an awesome time!"

The second thing I say, of course, is to—as Scar from Disney's *The Lion King* once ominously sang—*Be Prepared*. It really isn't so ominous in this case, just ensure you have a plan, that's all. Sure, you could go to Disney World for the day and just wing it but, if you really want to make the most out of your visit and maximize your opportunities to see as much of the stuff that's most important to you, especially if you're only there for one day, you must have a plan. Do your homework. Research height requirements for the rides you want to ride, especially if you have young kids. Decide if you want to take the time to eat at one of the more formal on-property restaurants, such as the *Beauty and the Beast* themed Be Our Guest Restaurant. If you do, keep in mind reservations start 180 days in advance, but also remember that you have to be willing to carve out a big chunk of time too because the full dining experience takes about 90 minutes. It also features a meet and greet experience with the Beast, so if you have young kids, consider if this may be too scary for them.

Do you want to watch the fireworks in front of Cinderella Castle? If so, plan an earlier dinner because you'll need to camp out in front of the castle for about an hour or so before they start and so you'll want to make sure to eat first. Festival of Fantasy parade is at 3:00 p.m., so if you want to see it, plan to be in the Main Street, USA area about 15 minutes before, and don't book any fast passes for rides during the 2:30-3:30 p.m. window, okay?

See what I mean? This is why I always start with, "Just relax and know you'll have fun no matter what," because it *can* be overwhelming to prepare that much for something that is supposed to be a whimsical and "footloose and fancy-free" experience. Just like anything in life, a little bit of preparation on the front end can save yourself a lot of disappointment in the end. By the way, I laid it on pretty thick up there for a reason—to further emphasize the importance of preparation, just in case you wondered if I actually was writing a Disney book there for a minute. No, it helped to hammer home the point that preparation will prove to be the key in all phases of life.

The other thing you may be wondering, since I chose to list the two words separately in this chapter's title, is what is the difference between preparation and preparedness and why did I feel the need to include both? I look at preparation as the "homework" I mentioned that entails the efforts you put in before you attempt to achieve a task—studying and researching ahead of time. Preparedness, on the other hand, again in my own view, is actually being prepared—both mentally and physically.

The "physical" part is why I included it as a separate lesson in this chapter. Let me explain. I mentioned in an earlier chapter that the key accompaniment for a trip to the Everglades, for example, was plenty of bug-spray. This, to me, is a good example of being physically prepared. It doesn't involve a ton of prework or research (or preparation), it is simply a matter of being prepared (or preparedness). If we look back to the example that I used to open this chapter, it would be like the presenter showing up that day without his laptop.

The reason why I think it warrants its own separate lesson, and, thus, why I made a point to distinguish the two, is because I think it's an easier thing to overlook. If you know you have a big test tomorrow, chances are you won't forget to study. But you might forget to bring your pencil. (Note, I said "if you know" you have a big test. If you don't remember you have one, you may just be *realy* screwed and end up with a 0/25).

This, too, is another lesson I learned during my outings. Saying I "learned" it may be a stretch. Of course, at this point in my career, I would hopefully not show up to an important meeting without my laptop with me. So, maybe I should say this story helped reinforce this lesson, which is just as important because sometimes we need to be reminded of these things that often seem fairly obvious.

One time, my kids and I were at a park that is nearby, still in Broward County, and about 20 minutes away, in Hollywood. This is the same park where I successfully observed the Blue-Crowned Parakeets earlier in the summer. Within minutes of being there on this visit, I went to take a photo of a bird that caught my eye, and, truth be told, I don't remember what it was.

As I pressed the button to snap a photo…nothing. I looked at the LCD screen on the camera, to see "please recharge battery," staring back at me. So, while I can say, with some degree of confidence, I would never forget my laptop if I were heading to an important meeting where I was presenting, not having my charger with me isn't out of the realm of possibility.

The only positive to this story, other than the lesson it helped to reinforce, is at least this didn't happen when I was in Jupiter that one day, some 90 minutes away, when I was on the prowl for a specific bird. Because after that one time in Hollywood when it happened, I've never let it happen since.

The simplicity of this lesson shouldn't be taken for granted because no matter how seasoned of an executive you are or how many times you've presented in front of large audiences, it is still a very good idea to double check that you're prepared for the next one. Whether it's a physical checklist or you're disciplined enough to do it in your head, it certainly doesn't hurt to take this extra step to ensure you don't have any snags (no, not pine ones) before the presentation even begins.

As it relates to preparation, this one is also easy to take for granted. But since I have spent my career in roles that require thorough planning and preparation from a communications standpoint, I'll offer some additional guidance as it relates to the importance of thinking through all outcomes. When

I sit down with an executive, for example, and start talking through "key messages" associated with a particular initiative we are communicating, especially if the news may be somewhat negative anyway—for example, a reorganization, one of the first things I'll encourage that executive to do, is think through how the words could be perceived by the audience.

Is there anything in here that could be construed as insensitive? Is there anything that could lead to even more questions, more uncertainty, more angst, or uneasiness, etc.? Are we unintentionally leaving too much to interpretation? Do we think this sentence here might lead to unnecessary panic?

This concept of thinking ahead is a hallmark of one of the brands I worked for specifically at Marriott—The Ritz-Carlton Hotel Company. The Ladies and Gentlemen of The Ritz-Carlton pride themselves on proactive service, anticipating the needs of their guests and offering services before the guest has a chance to ask. Sometimes, before the guests even realizes it themselves that they need something. You see someone returning to the hotel after a jog on the beach, looking a little sweaty or out of breath? "Here, sir. Here is a bottle of water and a towel." Someone appears to be a little lost and looking for one of the hotel's dining outlets or maybe the spa? "Hello, ma'am. Can I offer my assistance and help you find something?"

Looking for, and thinking through, scenarios, can help

you in all facets of life by anticipating potential outcomes and planning for them as a result.

Certainly, you may not be able to think through or plan for every single scenario, but you can do your best and mitigate as much of the potential backlash as you can, by thoroughly thinking through and preparing for as many of those scenarios as you can. The adage of "plan for the worst, hope for the best" rings true here. Any project manager would say to plan for the worst-case scenario and hopefully the preparation would be for naught. Think of it as buying car insurance and hoping you never have to use it.

Better yet, as I look at the eight cases of bottled water stacked on my dining room floor as I type this very sentence, ask any Floridian what hurricane preparation is like. Better to have 10,000 batteries in your coat closet than be sitting in the dark when the power goes out with flashlights that don't turn on.

Because you never know, and that's why you prepare.

It would have been awesome to have spotted that Red-Headed Woodpecker within moments of us pulling into that park on that miserably hot Friday afternoon, but you can't assume that will happen without doing the proper amount of preparation first, to increase your likelihood of success.

So, go ahead and learn what a Red-Headed Woodpecker sounds like, before you leave the house and go to look for one.

Chapter 8

PRESENCE, FOCUS, AND PAYING ATTENTION: THE BLUE-GRAY GNATCATCHER

"Ice cream for breakfast? Whose bright idea was that?"
— Me

The Blue-gray Gnatcatcher taken August 2020 at Plantation Preserve, Plantation, Florida.

Have you ever been sitting at your desk at home (or dining room table in my case), checking some emails and scrolling through the morning's headlines on the news site of your choice, when one of your kids comes up to ask you a question? You say, "Sure, what's up?" without even taking your eyes off your screen for a second. You know you're *hearing* them talking, but truth be told, you're not really *listening* to what they're saying. And yes, there is a difference.

If you're lucky, you may catch every third word. Still, this doesn't stop you from firing off a somewhat dismissive, "Yeah, that sounds good," as you continue your business. About 10 minutes later, you walk into the kitchen to fill up your coffee mug for the second time to see your kid standing at the counter, scooping ice cream, and helping himself to his own version of the "breakfast of champions" at 9:00 a.m.

"Whoa, bud. What is this all about?"

"You told me I could, dad."

"Yeah, right. Keep dreaming. When?"

"Like, 10 minutes ago."

You retrace your steps in your head and think, "Darn, *that's* what he asked? I kind of remember hearing the words 'ice cream' but I assumed he meant for dessert tonight."

Even if nothing this egregious comes to mind, chances are you've been guilty of this sort of in-between state of being physically present and yet, your mind has other ideas. Because "presence" as used in this chapter, is more than simply being there. It requires an intentional effort where your mind is also in the same place as your body physically is. A lot of our inattentiveness can be a natural byproduct of the "cluttered schedule" phenomenon I spoke of earlier. But we don't do ourselves any favors, nor our kids for that matter—and I'll expound upon this later in the chapter—when we put ourselves in a situation where our own inability to remove distractions, even for just a moment, hinders our ability to focus on one thing at a time.

I've seen variations of the same meme floating around social media for years which states "I'm now at the point where I find myself turning down the radio while driving so I can see better." While people post these sorts of things for the laughs, and they usually get them, because "Duh, we don't use our ears to see." I've forever refuted the premise of this message and recently shared this fact when a close friend posted this same meme a few months ago. I said that I am one of the people who routinely does this, but it is not to *see* better, it's to *focus* better. If I am driving somewhere, particularly at night or somewhere unfamiliar, adding the distraction of music interferes with me trying to concentrate and focus on the core task at hand—driving.

My response seemed to generate a lot of, "Yeah, sure Matt," type replies but to me this doesn't seem like such a strange or difficult concept to grasp. At least, it shouldn't be. It would be like turning down the same loud radio if someone came in the room to ask you a question or because you decided to read a book instead. Anything that requires higher levels of focus such as, I don't know, safely arriving at your destination, may mean that sometimes any other potential distraction needs to be removed.

There is a famous scene in the 1984 film, *The Karate Kid,* where Mr. Miyagi, portrayed by the late Pat Morita, is kneeling in front of a coffee table, intently staring at a fly buzzing around him as he repeatedly grasps at it with a pair of chopsticks. Daniel, played by Ralph Macchio, inadvertently distracts his sensei, and ever so slightly breaks Miyagi's concentration when he shows up and sits down next to him. Still, Miyagi never takes his eyes off the fly, not even to say hello, which suggests he is trying his best to focus on what appears to be a task that requires as much of it as possible. Perhaps feeling the need to break an awkward silence, Daniel asks, "Wouldn't a fly swatter be easier?" Miyagi replies that a man who can accomplish this task, can accomplish anything, before he reveals that he's never caught one before. Daniel then asks if he can try and on his fourth attempt, snatches a fly out of the air, at which point Miyagi tosses his chopsticks aside and storms off.

I chose to reference this scene for a couple reasons. First, it helps to reinforce the lesson that will be the focus of this chapter on focus (see what I did there?), and, secondly, it also reinforces the fact that, sometimes, there are exceptions to every rule. Daniel catching this fly, as Miyagi correctly points out, is simply a case of "beginner's luck." Not unlike my example with the Night Heron and how sometimes you get lucky even if you don't "put in the time."

Another interesting thing about this scene is that when I first thought about including it in this book, I had planned to put it in the chapter on patience. Sure, one could argue that this task also requires extraordinary patience, and it does but more importantly, it requires focus. "Undivided attention," to quote every elementary school teacher in America. I have come to interpret that this scene is meant to illustrate that it is not enough to be patient, you need to commit every ounce of focus and concentration on the task at hand to have a realistic shot of accomplishing said task. Because Miyagi did, in fact, remain patient with Daniel and himself, but it was his focus that was compromised.

Like the example of the father (or mother—why do we assume it is always the dad?) granting permission for his kid to eat ice cream for breakfast, Miyagi was still physically sitting in the same spot, but his mental presence was elsewhere just enough to impede his own chances of attaining success.

The only thing that would have been more distracting for Mr. Miyagi, is if a second fly appeared, and then a third. You might assume that this would actually increase his chances but not quite. This is a lesson I learned not too long ago because birding oftentimes requires the same level of focus, especially when you are attempting to observe and photograph a small warbler as I discussed earlier when talking about Ovenbirds. However, perhaps the peskiest of all these smaller fall migrants is fittingly named, the Blue-gray Gnatcatcher.

If you're not familiar with this bird, your imagination is likely doing a good job on its own. A bird that feasts on gnats, which are clearly pesky in their own right, must not only be tiny, but shifty enough to be able to catch enough of them, and do so often enough to survive. In truth, despite the name, they usually will eat smaller insects and spiders. Still, they are incredibly small, the smallest of the species I've attempted to observe thus far.

What makes attempting to photograph a Gnatcatcher even more challenging than it sounds is that usually, to find one, you cannot simply look for the bird alone. You must pay attention and try to find other clues first, such as looking for rustling leaves that could indicate something is there, as well as using other senses to listen for signs of life, too. And, you have to stay attentive and focused on that area the entire time—again, patience being required—because looking away for even a split second can be costly.

While most lessons in this book are based on one specific incident or outing, this one is not. Because, even though I am now cognizant of this fact, I cannot tell you the number of times I will walk past a tree while wandering through a place such as Plantation Preserve and notice something fluttering in that same tree that compels, if not forces, me to stop and inspect. As I do so and stand there waiting to look and listen for more clues, I catch something out of the periphery that, in much the same way the original fluttering did just moments earlier, forces me to turn my head to the left (or right) in an attempt to see what it is. Then, I may hear something behind me, so I'll turn around on instinct to see what *that* may have been.

Both moves prove to be a mistake, of course, because I allowed not only one, but two, outside distractions to break my concentration just enough when I was trying to observe my original target. Since I didn't have a good view of either of the two other "things" to begin with, and I never actually saw anything at all, and was distracted only by a noise, by the time I returned my focus back to that original spot, it was too late. Whatever it was, also, is now gone. So, three birds (potentially) right around me, and I didn't even see one, let alone have an opportunity to photograph it. If the old bird cliché I used in chapter 2, "A bird in the hand is worth two in the bush," is true, then a bird right in front of us, ready to be photographed, is worth *more than* three flying around us at the same time.

It can be incredibly tempting to do this, too, don't get me wrong. Especially if I'm observing that original spot for five minutes or so, and something behind me appears to be louder and thus leads me to believe it provides a more likely chance for a successful outcome. In hindsight, perhaps it's not a bad thing that this has happened to me several times, because it makes the lesson much more profound in many ways. In fact, I think it makes the lesson even more important, too, because it illustrates just how easily we allow ourselves to be distracted, no matter how conscientious we are about not letting it happen.

I've said before, and will continue to say, that one of the most rewarding aspects of this activity is being able to be alone with your own thoughts as you wander along these nature trails with not even the sound of cars in the distance providing unnecessary distractions. Certainly not the sound of the television, and dare I say, children who are doing nothing wrong other than what kids sometimes do—be loud. Some of my most treasured moments, as well as the most important moments, were those times I found myself almost lost in my own thoughts, which gave me the opportunity to process the things weighing most heavily on my mind at the time—such as another job that didn't work out or wondering how much longer I could afford to be out of work before I seriously needed to start thinking of alternatives.

All this alone time was extraordinarily critical, and perhaps the biggest benefit of all, because it allowed me, if not forced me, to not only acknowledge my feelings but process them, too. It gave me time I wouldn't otherwise

The Black-and-white Warbler, Sept. 2020, Plantation, Fla.

have had. However, when it came time to set my sights on a Gnatcatcher or a Black-and-white Warbler, allowing my mind to wander while in pursuit of these species would sabotage my ability to successfully photograph one. I had to quickly adjust and know when to make that pivot and "get back in the zone."

This is a lesson and a skill we need to keep top of mind in all aspects of our life, too, whether at work, which I'll share more thoughts on later in the chapter, or at home. Otherwise, our kids end up with a bowl of ice cream at 9:00 in the morning, or worse, as I'll explain soon.

As I said, we are all guilty of this. Or, I should say, I assume many are. A spouse, a child, a friend, etc., could be talking to us, and even if we aren't distracted by a device, we oftentimes are distracted by the thoughts swirling in our own head.

I'll be honest. Kristie, for example, will say something to me once in a while, such as, "Hey, remember I have an appointment tomorrow evening, so can you take Emma to gymnastics?" and I'll look at her somewhat puzzled and think to myself, "Remember? Umm no. News to me." But as it usually turns out, she likely *did* tell me days, if not weeks, before. But guess what? I wouldn't be able to tell you because it was probably another one of those "Yeah, sure sounds good" scenarios.

That brings me back to the point I started to make above. Not only are we setting ourselves up for failure by allowing ourselves, even if unintentionally, to be distracted while talking to others, especially a child, but think of the message that then sends to them. Of course, it should also be said that perhaps our kids should be a little more polite, too, if they see us working but they're kids. Either way, sending the message, even subliminally, that "you are not worth my time" is not only rude, but could be incredibly damaging, too. If it is a common recurrence, it reinforces that same subliminal message again and again that just about anything else in your life takes priority over them.

The topics our kids come to us with sometimes are, let's just say, not very interesting. To us. To them, it's the most important thing in the world, at that moment anyway. By unintentionally signaling to them that we don't care about their interests, it also could send the signal we don't care about them, either. Not to be dramatic, it's just something to think about the next time your child starts to drone on about Fortnite or an American Girl doll accessory.

I mentioned earlier that I took the Enneagram personality that suggested I was an "enthusiast" because I had a lot of varied interests before I ever thought birding would be among them. A few years ago, Kristie and I took one of those tests together, which you may have heard of, based on the book of the same name by Gary Chapman called *The Five Love Languages,* which is meant to help you better understand the needs of your spouse. The premise is that the things that matter to you are not necessarily the things that matter to someone else, particularly your other (i.e., better) half.

For Kristie, one of her top scores was "Quality Time." I wouldn't always understand why, but if we were even sitting together watching a movie on the couch, if I was multitasking by checking a quick score of a football game, or browsing a social media site, it would bother her or, more accurately, hurt her feelings. I'd say, "We're *just* watching television. What does it matter? It's not like we are engaging in a meaningful discussion or something."

I eventually learned, however, that regardless of the activity—even one such as watching television—if we are doing that activity together, and she felt I wasn't as invested in it as

I should be, then it could be taken as a sign that I didn't care about spending time with her, and, even worse, I didn't care or acknowledge that it *was i*mportant to her, even if it wasn't to me. So, again, the need to show someone you're focused on just one thing—them—implies that you do, indeed, care.

Conversely, my language was "Words of Affirmation," which essentially means that I like to hear positive words from others to feel "loved." So, back to my earlier point above about having someone share something that is interesting to them, only to feel the brush off—if this were to happen to me, I know it would hurt my feelings, too. If, for example, I was excited to share a chapter I had just written for this book, and the other person gave me a "Hey, that's great" type of response while juggling a million other things, I would feel, at the very least, deflated, if not discouraged.

In either case, showing someone that you're committed to focusing on them, and only them, in that moment can have the opposite effect. It could make them feel valued, special, important, and appreciated.

This is a good opportunity to transition to work, as I alluded to earlier. I once had a boss, Heather, who—regardless of what she was doing—if I knocked on her door, which was open, and as a courtesy I'd ask, "Do you have a second," once I was in her office, she'd turn her computer monitor off. I observed this time and time again, and it's not because it was facing me, and she didn't want me to see potentially confidential information. It was facing her, and I acknowledged this once after observing it for several months.

Heather's response, which I remember vividly nearly 15 years later, was because she didn't want to give the perception that anything was more important in that moment than listening to one of her employees who needed help or had a question. On top of that, because like many of us, if she saw or heard a "ding" that signaled an incoming email, she'd be prone to glance at it and potentially allow herself to be distracted by it, which again, could be taken as a sign that I wasn't important enough for her time.

John Maxwell, a well-known leadership expert, once stated that the greatest thing a leader can do for the people on their team, is to treat the person they are talking to as though they are not only the most important person in the world at that moment, but the only one. "Set aside your agenda—if you want to connect with other people, you must make their agenda your priority in that moment," Maxwell stated in a recent blog. That is such a powerful way to look at it.

This applies in situations in the workplace that aren't one-on-one meetings, too. I've shared throughout this book, some mistakes I made either as a student in school or as a young professional learning the ropes of the business world. I said that

I couldn't recall anything overtly inappropriate, rather some faux pas that could have unintended consequences. This anecdote falls into this category. Earlier in my career, I was "guilty" of checking email on my—not to date myself—BlackBerry while in a meeting. I could spin it to say that I was always very conscientious and committed to responding quickly. However, I neglected to consider the subtle, or not-so-subtle, impression I was giving to those in the room, including, on occasion, my boss.

I am thankful that one of them pulled me aside one day to point this out and do so in a constructive manner. Again, he even positioned it the way I described above in that he knew it came from a place where I thought I was simply being as responsive as I could be to those trying to email me with a request but also shared the perception it gives others in the room, that my focus is not with them or on them. He, of course, was not only referring to himself, but future bosses who might not be as forgiving or understanding.

In the beginning, I found myself having to leave my phone at my desk if I didn't trust myself enough to leave it in my pocket, which is fine. If you need to employ various tactics to ensure your focus can't waver—at least because of the device in your pocket—then that's certainly acceptable. I am grateful he pulled me aside that day, and, even more so, that he did it with the goal of giving me good advice for the future as opposed to making me feel reprimanded, although he wouldn't have been wrong to take that approach.

Perhaps your organization or current boss doesn't frown upon these sorts of things but if you find that you, too, are inclined to become distracted by having your iPhone with you, then consider trying similar approaches.

The same can be true when it comes to goal setting at work. If you remember the visual of Mr. Miyagi trying to catch three flies at once, I took a training session years ago delivered by a Franklin-Covey facilitator and author, Jim Huling, where this concept comes into play. Huling and two colleagues, Chris McChesney and Sean Covey, created what they refer to as the *Four Disciplines of Execution* and published a book with this same title. This is essentially a four-step approach to more effective goal setting, and the first step is "Focus on The Wildly Important." They coined the term WIG or, Wildly Important Goal. "Exceptional execution starts with narrowing the focus—clearly identifying what must be done, or nothing else you achieve really matters much," as Huling stated.

In Huling's talk that day, which incidentally was at The Ritz-Carlton in Tysons Corner, Virginia, where he was facilitating the session for the hotel's leadership team, he asked the group if you are better off setting 10 goals for yourself or two. Many people said 10, thinking that showed a "go get 'em" attitude. As Huling pointed out, focusing on so many "priorities" means you're probably giving each of the 10 partial focus and thus will likely end up with either mediocre results. Or worse, you'll potentially fail to reach even one of your goals, just like trying to see three Gnatcatchers instead of one.

By the way, since I've picked on the iPhone throughout this chapter, and will again, I'll balance the scales here a little when I say one of my favorite quotes on this philosophy belongs to Apple CEO, Tim Cook. Cook said the following at a Goldman Sachs conference in 2009. "We say no to good ideas every day. We say no to *great* ideas in order to keep the amount of things we focus on very small in number, so that we can put enormous energy behind the ones we do choose, so that we can deliver the best products in the world."

Think about this. If I thought turning my head to find a new bird was tempting, Apple, arguably the most innovative company in the world, must resist this same temptation every single day. It requires a concerted effort and disciplined rigidity to do this.

That's not to say you need to be so rigid all the time. Like what I said about knowing when to pivot from having your mind wander while looking for birds, to focusing intently if you wanted to see one, you'll have to use your best judgment, based on your personal circumstances, to know when it's okay to multitask and when not to. Hint: when your spouse comes up to you and says, "Can we talk," this is *not* one of those times, unless you have a comfortable couch.

Now is a good time to point out that birdwatching doesn't *always* require this level of focus either. You can certainly take a leisurely stroll through Plantation Preserve, look up only occasionally, and see a handful of pretty spectacular things. However, to achieve "next-level results," just know that checking your iPhone every 30 seconds as you try to spot a Blue-gray Gnatcatcher amid dense foliage will prove to be a rather futile effort.

In fact, on a more recent visit with my own dear mother, I had to politely tell her to hush at one point because, yes, even a friendly chat with my mom can be enough of a distraction to hinder my ability to find an elusive bird. Sometimes that's just fine, because there are, of course, instances our walks and chats take precedent over anything else. Going back to earlier statements about realizing birding is more than just "padding my stats," being able to spend quality time with my mom—or kids in other instances—is often the most important part of it.

The point is, though, as is the case with anything in life, whether or not you choose to give something your full focus and attention is up to you. If you want to reach the pinnacle of success in anything, that can't happen without focusing and giving your full attention to it, even if it's becoming harder and harder to do that.

I once worked with a gentleman, Adam, who earned his PhD in organizational psychology. He hadn't done any sort of study on this particular topic but based on his own observations on both workplace and household trends, said that "multitasking" is no longer a thing and that he replaced the term with "continuous partial attention." His premise is that due to a variety of circumstances (iPhones, as well as the "20 balls in the air" effect covered earlier), we are no longer able to focus fully on only one thing at a time. Ever. Further, he suggests the more adept we are at being able to thrive in this world of ever-present distractions, the better off we will be, but we need to first accept this as our new reality and then be okay with it.

To some degree, he may be right. There will be many times when giving continuous partial attention to several things at once is in fact the best, if not only, way to get it all done. Cooking dinner while dancing around the kitchen to get your cardio in as you listen to an audiobook that is required for your job, all while you watch the dog roam around the backyard, hoping he doesn't get loose because that'll have to be a suitable substitute for the walk you usually take him on as you give your kids pop quizzes with the flash cards on the counter next to the recipe, you're using to make dinner. Just be sure not to mistakenly put 100 teaspoons of salt in your meal after shouting, "What's 50x2?" to your child in the other room.

Does it have to be this way? *All* the time? I don't think it does, and shudder to think we are past the point where being able to focus on one thing at a time is beyond the realm of possibility. Birding not only reminded me that it doesn't always have to be this way, but it made me realize that it couldn't be if I wanted to give myself a half-decent chance to be able to find those flurrying feathered friends flying, fluttering, and flapping far away. (Sorry, that didn't start out with such alliteration, but I was on a roll). It then it forced me to shift away from this mindset and, despite the numerous distractions that have become so commonplace in our lives, we need to do whatever it takes to not be pulled away by them when we can't afford to be.

One additional point on presence. I believe this is equally important when it comes to attending your kids' sporting events, school plays, and dance recitals, too. It should be stated that there are times when work or other responsibilities prohibit us from attending every single event, and that's not what I am suggesting. I've missed my fair share of baseball games and school assemblies for work commitments and the occasional business trip. But if you are going to be there, then try your best to *be* there. Scrolling on your phone or reading a book isn't exactly being present.

I'm sure I've been guilty of this but not very often. I'm not patting myself on the back, either. It's mainly because I've either been a coach such as with my boys' flag football teams, and because, for every baseball team they've been on, if I wasn't volunteering to help coach, I was volunteering to keep the scorebook. For one, I have always loved to do that but, two, much like I had to keep my phone at my desk at work to stop me from wanting to check it during a meeting, keeping score for a baseball game is a mechanism that ensured I'd pay attention to every pitch, and not just when my kids were at bat. If you don't think it matters to your kids if you miss their big hit in the bottom of the last inning by accident because you didn't realize his turn was approaching, don't ask me. Ask them.

The other secondary lesson, which is called out in the title of this chapter for a reason, and I briefly touched on it when I first mentioned the Gnatcatcher, is that "paying attention" doesn't only mean looking intently at something or *for* something. As mentioned, this also generally requires you to lean on and rely upon other senses in your "toolkit," and use them to your advantage.

Earlier in the school year, Dylan was listening to an audio article for science class, and since he knew I'd find it interesting, he excitedly wanted to share it. Not to get too tangential but now that I think about it, if our kids have the wherewithal to share something with *us*, they know is important to us, then conversely, we owe it to our kids to demonstrate this same ability when they share something that is important to *them*, too. In any case, the article was about how birds use several different strategies and tactics and rely on their various senses to find food.

Herons and egrets, which I have discussed before, rely on sight foremost. They will sit there staring at the water for lengthy periods of time, looking for fish. Wood Storks, which also feed primarily on fish, will plunge their beaks into the water to "look for" their next meal because presumably their eyesight isn't as keen as that of a Heron. Or maybe like me before I discovered birding, they aren't as patient. White Ibises on the other hand, can often be seen with their curved bills hovering just so slightly above the ground because they use their bills to find food. Every other step or so, they can be seen pecking at the ground to help them find it by feeling it.

What a fitting analogy. I'll take a page from their book to emphasize this lesson, which is we need to use a few different strategies of our own when it comes to being able to fully "pay attention."

To keep the analogy going, when our kids come to us to talk, as a parent it is also up to us to proactively look for other nonverbal cues that could potentially signal something is on their mind. Are they sitting at the dinner table pushing their food back and forth without taking a bite? Do they spend an excessive amount of time wanting to be alone and seem extra moody? By paying attention to these kinds of things, it allows us to connect with our children and identify if something bigger is truly on their mind as opposed to not being hungry that night because they had a later lunch.

There are expressions we use such as "trusting your gut" or something "passing the sniff test." These are examples of how we can use our senses and our intuition to observe and pay attention to things that we would not be able to observe if we walk into our kids' rooms with our face buried in an iPhone. If something is up, you'll be glad you did.

As I shared in chapter 5, our time is precious. We can all commit to spending that time focused on *what* we should be, *when* we should be, and, preferably, one thing at a time, because trying to see three Blue-gray Gnatcatcher instead of one will leave you empty handed in the end.

Chapter 9

PERSPECTIVE: THE NORTHERN MOCKINGBIRD AND THE INDIGO BUNTING

"Matthew, what is it you keep staring at out there? Searching for the meaning of life?"– My Father, John

"In some ways, yes."— Me

The Northern Mockingbird taken in my backyard, May 2020 in Plantation, Florida.

This is a chapter and a lesson that has two meanings. Two perspectives on perspective, if you will. As in the case with time, one of the two has a more practical application to it and the other a little more philosophical. There is, however, some overlap where both principles intersect.

Let's start out with the more practical take on this concept, and this is where I look at perspective purely in the physical sense. Meaning, to observe something—a bird for instance—in its truest form, you must sometimes change your physical perspective to do so.

I'd like to share a story of two gentlemen who dedicated more than 10 years of their lives in search of rare and unobserved species in Papua, New Guinea, known as the Birds of Paradise—National Geographic photographer Tim Laman and Cornell University ornithologist Edwin Scholes.

As noted throughout this book, my love of all things Disney has been well documented. I subscribed to Disney+, the company's streaming service when it became available last year. At first, I used it primarily to watch classic animated movies and new Disney-specific programs exclusive to this new platform. Over the last several months, however, I have found myself skipping straight to the section that features National Geographic content, which became part of the Disney portfolio after its acquisition of 20th Century Fox a couple years ago. This includes, by the way, the documentary on Everglades National Park that Dylan and I watched last spring for his class. (I still love Mickey, it's just that I am making room for more "friends" now—such as the Birds of Paradise).

Toward the end of August, I stumbled upon the aforementioned documentary officially known as *Winged Seduction: Birds of Paradise*, produced in 2012. As the Disney+ description states, these birds are "shape-shifting, dancing, dazzling transformers," each more spectacular than the next. I've since watched it several times and even ordered the book—yet another addition to the growing bird library—based on it and filled with dozens of Laman's brilliant pictures. The documentary itself is fascinating, and the concept of physical perspective is at its core.

In one of the stories in particular, Scholes and Laman were attempting to observe a species they had already been successful observing once, but they needed a perspective that would answer unknown questions that could only be answered by physically changing the way they photographed and filmed this specific bird—a Carola's Parotia. As is the case with all the Birds of Paradise species, the males are recognized as being the more flamboyant, exotic, and, frankly, more beautiful between the two genders but beyond that, the Parotia, specifically, is known for performing an intricate and almost bizarre dance that seems to be choreographed with such extreme precision and part of the courtship ritual to attract a female mate.

Both Laman and Scholes had seen this before but to fully understand it, they needed to look at it from the physical perspective of the female being courted. The dance seemed random and nonsensical to them but perhaps they were missing something that only this other vantagepoint could answer.

After they successfully found the location of the court, which was an ordeal in itself, Laman and Scholes set up three different cameras, a mix of both video and still photography, from three different angles. Including one hovering from above, which provided what Scholes described as the "holy grail" view of the dance—the female view.

Patience, again, was the name of the game. Two days after they arrived back on one of the most remote parts of what is already a remote island, Scholes and Laman successfully observed, and using the three cameras, documented for the first time in history, this unique perspective that finally made them realize there was more to the dance than initially assumed. It revealed things they otherwise would never have known, and neither would the rest of the world, such as the male parotia has a yellowish hidden patch under black plumage that he "flashes" at one point in the dance, and it can only be seen from above, from—to borrow the phrase—*a bird's eye view.* This proved to be the missing piece for the dance to make more sense.

This is not only a perfect example of the importance of physical perspective, but also an incredible exhibition of so many of the other things I've talked about throughout this book—passion, perseverance, patience, and putting in time and miles. It also touches on things I will discuss later, such as continuing to pursue excellence, because even after they successfully observed and photographed this once-in-a-lifetime species—one 99 percent of the birding community, I'd venture to say, will never have the chance to see—it wasn't good enough for them.

Throughout the documentary, Scholes and Laman share other anecdotes of the hurdles they have had to jump over—literally—to gain better perspective. Laman shared that he once climbed 50 meters in a tree, and hovered there for hours, just for the chance to see a rare bird. Passion, patience, perseverance, perspective, and clearly no fear of heights.

Bringing it down a level—or 100—I, too, have discovered the importance of physical perspective when it comes to my own birding endeavors. I've shared a few surface-level examples already. For instance, the American Redstart, who was hidden behind a bunch of dense leaves. There are other examples—a lot in fact—where I have seen a bird I was attempting to photograph in plain sight, and because I didn't have a good enough or optimum physical perspective, photographing it seemed to be as futile as looking for the Blue-gray Gnatcatcher while doing three other things.

Any photographer, along with anyone like me—someone with a pretty nice camera who enjoys taking pictures—can share stories where the light just wasn't right, the settings just weren't to be found, no matter how much you tinkered with things such as shutter speed, aperture, and ISO, which relates to the camera's sensitivity to light. You can take a ton of beautiful photos by using the "automatic" settings on your camera regardless of the brand, but to capture more precise images, adjusting the manual settings of those three elements can help a lot but they aren't magic makers, either. Even popular and effective "post-production" editing programs, while they can help bring out the best in a photo and usually do, cannot do much when a photo is either blurry or the subject is completely dark. So, if the light isn't right, the bird is too high (unless you're willing to set up a vantage point 50 meters high), or the sky is too dark (or light), sometimes there isn't much to do about it.

Sometimes there is, though. Fairly simple things, such as taking pictures with the sun behind you instead of in front of you can help. Again, that's fairly simple, but since these birds are mobile, and some of them seemingly easily startled, even taking a few steps to ensure the sun is to your back, can be enough to make the bird fly off before you have an opportunity.

In some instances, and not unlike the parotia photographed by Laman and Scholes, I had to physically position myself to see the bird from a different perspective to fully appreciate it. The best example of this, that I photographed last summer, is the Red-winged Blackbird. A common resident of the Plantation Preserve over the summer, this is a bird

The Red-winged Blackbird, June 2020. Plantation, Fla.

that many might dismiss as being a common grackle or another generic "black bird" without much "beauty" to be found. Sure, there is beauty in all of them, as I've come to determine, but the truth is, some are less breathtaking than others—at least less colorful anyway. Thus, the first time I saw one of these, I was surprised and then quickly delighted to discover changing my physical perspective revealed something entirely different.

Speaking of grackles, this Boat-tailed Grackle I photographed on my fortieth birthday in June, is another example of perspective. When the sun hits just right, the plain black coat reveals a glowing iridescence that one can easily miss. Another example of what happens when you see things from a different lens.

Sometimes, though, it doesn't matter what we do, and I learned that during my summer road trip I referenced earlier. I've shared some tidbits about the stop to visit my brother and his family in Tallahassee. Our week in Delaware to visit my dad and stepmom, Wendy, who had moved there last spring after my dad retired following a 44-year career with the federal government, was the primary reason for the trip. Tallahassee isn't exactly next door, but given it is seven hours away and in the same state, it's safe to say it won't be a one-time trip. The ability to drive to Delaware might be.

When my dad first pitched the idea to me about driving there, around the middle of May, knowing it was a rare opportunity for me to have the time to do so, I was excited to see him and Wendy of course, and to be close to the beaches in the mid-Atlantic I grew up visiting—namely Ocean City, Maryland. I vacationed there every summer, usually fitting in several visits between June and September. The vacations with my parents looked a little different than the ones with my friends in my early 20s, but maybe those stories are for future books.

As the trip to see my dad drew closer, I also realized that those same birds I just missed since discovering birding at the end of spring migration were, by mid-July, visiting their summer homes, some of which were in Delaware.

Over the course of the week, I saw and photographed

dozens that I hadn't been able to see in Florida yet, including an American Goldfinch, American Robin, and some of the "gulls" that are more common to the Eastern Shore than they are to the Florida coast. Another highlight "lifer"

The American Goldfinch, July 2020. Millville, Del.

sighting that week was an Eastern Bluebird, which holds special meaning for our family and has for as long as I can remember because of my mom's mother, my Grandma (Wilma), who lives near us in South Florida. At 89-years-old, she is as much a part of my kids' lives as any grandparent or great-grandparent could be and was a big part of my life growing up, too.

My Grandma has been famous for giving "Blue Birds of Happiness" to people as gifts over the years. I have one as does each of my kids, and it's safe to say many members of my family have theirs as well. A family of bluebirds that will live on for generations, thanks to my grandmother. They are beautifully handcrafted glass ornaments, and I've always loved mine but now it makes

The Eastern Bluebird, July 2020. Millville, Del.

me smile even more after I saw a real living Eastern Bluebird for the first time during this trip. One of the photos I took of it sits beside the glass one from my grandmother in my curio cabinet in my family room.

One more thing to add about my grandmother. Talk about someone whose hardships help you gain perspective. She lost a son to cancer when he was 16 years old—my late uncle, Stevie, whom I unfortunately never got to meet but am told I look just like. How people can go through something so traumatic and still go on with their life is beyond me, but another reminder of perspective. What's also worth noting is that my mom, despite losing her brother when she herself was a teenager in 1972, has maintained a positive outlook on life after dealing with such a profound tragedy during what should've been some of the best years of her life as she prepared for college. The strength of both my mother and grandmother, is yet another example of why we should be grateful for each new day, each new chance to experience something new.

Back to my dad's house and another "blue" bird that was not as easy for me to see that week, which serves as the basis for this next story on perspective. Often, especially in situations where your physical perspective doesn't allow for it, you'll hear many more birds than you'll be able to see. My dad's lot backed into two groupings of tall trees with a large field situated in between the two groupings. His backyard was separated from these trees and the field by a very shallow creek that prevented me from crossing over it to get closer to the trees and stand in the open field. But I could hear dozens of birds in those trees that kept me wondering what they might be.

I wasn't that familiar with calls just yet but between the book Wendy owned on the birds of the Mid-Atlantic (like mine for Florida), along with some other research I was doing while there, I convinced myself there were Indigo Buntings living in some of the trees I was staring at every morning as I drank my coffee on the patio, and every evening when I sat there enjoying a cocktail, too. It turned out I was right.

In the early morning hours, when many in the house were asleep, and when it felt that the rest of the world was too, I'd gaze at the field for hours, compelling my father to ask, "Matthew, what is it you keep staring at out there? Searching for the meaning of life?"

"In some ways, yes," I said.

Closely related to the Painted Bunting I've referenced before, and a member of the Cardinal family, the Indigo Bunting is another species I would not be able to see in Florida any time soon. So, I was excited. Especially when I made this discovery early in the week, thinking that was more than enough time. In fact, more time I had than in any other birding trip to date.

Driving 90 minutes to see a Crested Caracara, then taking a couple hours for it to happen was likely the most time spent thus far. Here, I had a week. Just call me Mr. Scholes, thank you very much!

Despite how close I was able to get (which wasn't close enough), the light, the settings, and other variables never aligned in the right way. I won't show you the dozens of photos I took where the Indigo Bunting appeared to

The Indigo Bunting, July 2020. Millville, Del.

be masquerading as its cousin, the Gray and Grainy Bunting (I hope you can detect the sarcasm there, if not, I am losing my touch. Just to be sure, there is no such thing as a Gray and Grainy Bunting). I did, however, manage to capture this gem (more sarcasm) as I had, a couple times that week, seen one flutter by as I sat there staring at the field and trees. I observed this several times, but because of the physical distance created by that creek, I was never able to follow where he landed. In any case, for proof I saw one, and so I could add it to my eBird "lifer list" as a confirmed sighting—here it is, without further ado, the Indigo Bunting!

Being able, and willing, to change your physical perspective to see something better is, of course, an important lesson to learn and be mindful of in a wide variety of ways. "Willing" because when I said I couldn't cross that creek, truth be told, I could have. Anyone could have. Certainly, Scholes and Laman *would* have. Nevertheless, it's an important reminder that sometimes we must go to fairly significant lengths to change our physical perspective. Sometimes to the point we must sacrifice our comfort, like getting our feet and legs soaked by crossing a creek with who-knows-what living in it. As I'll share momentarily, sometimes we must go to similar lengths to change our mental perspective, too.

Since I've already mentioned Disney once this chapter, here's an example. If you are with your young children, standing in front of Cinderella Castle enjoying the fireworks, and one of your smaller kids complains that they cannot see, before you say something such as, "What do you mean? We have a great view!" Perhaps consider crouching down to their level first. Because you'll see things from—wait for it—*A Whole New World*. Theirs. This doesn't mean you now are free to have them sit on your shoulders, either. This, like me checking emails on my phone during a meeting, is a huge faux pas. But, if you can, try to hold them in your arms in a way so your heads are at the same height.

The same principle applies in many other situations but for the best examples of real-life applicability to perspective, it's time to shift gears to the second approach to perspective, and frankly, the more important one, especially given the environment today and the last several months specifically.

I consider myself extraordinarily grateful to have been given the opportunity to return to work, as I said in the preface. What I hadn't shared yet is that, despite me thinking it was not very likely, it was a return to Marriott. I am blessed to continue my journey with the company where I've spent the bulk of my career. This cannot be overstated. I am fortunate, thankful, and, yes, above all, grateful but I am also very sensitive to the fact that so many others, including former bosses and dozens of colleagues I worked closely with, and know personally, were not given this same opportunity. Many of them are still looking for their next door to open or, in my case *re-open*, as I've described it as. This doesn't include the countless others who are more than numbers and statistics, but people. Husbands, sons, brothers, fathers, wives, daughters, sisters, and mothers.

I've returned to work with a new perspective. The two-hour long conference calls I used to complain about are now met with the same gratitude I had when I accepted the role, as I realize the folks who are still out of work would probably give just about anything to be on one of those calls.

It needs to be clearly stated that we don't always have to *change* our perspective, or develop a new one, to still be able to see and understand someone else's. It may not necessarily change our perspective, but it may, in fact, still make us see things a little differently anyway. At the very least, it demonstrates compassion and empathy and is a sign of respect, and that's what the bulk of this lesson is focused on.

When I returned to work, I did so with a perspective based on the challenges faced during those several months away, challenges many of my colleagues who stayed with the company during those tough times did not have to experience. Challenges I'd never experienced before either. During my first meeting with my new boss, Blair, as well as her boss, Lance, in a separate meeting, they spent the first few minutes simply asking how I was doing and feeling and took the time to acknowledge me as a person before we jumped right in to "business as usual." I cannot tell you how much that meant to me, and then gave me the boost to pivot and get back to the grind.

It showed me, first and foremost, that even though they didn't share the same perspective, because how could they, they were willing to take the time to understand it, and it showed compassion which allowed them to gain empathy before they asked me to just dive right back in. It shouldn't take a pandemic to remind employers that when welcoming new teammates to their organization or welcoming back former employees who've been out of work for several months, that giving them just a few minutes to share their perspective on the challenges they've had to overcome can go a long way in their ability to bounce back quickly.

Knowing these two leaders, they would have done so regardless—they would have asked about me anyway, because that's who they are. Plus, treating employees as human beings has long since been one of the hallmarks of my company's culture but, by and large, we cannot afford to live in a world where we don't take the time to understand the perspective of others, whether at work or in our personal relationships. More on those in a second.

Another lesson is while Blair and Lance were not out of work, it doesn't mean they were immune to hardships during that time, not by any means. They had to work longer hours, were stretched thin, "holding down the fort," while at the same time having to say goodbye to colleagues and friends who, as I've said before, had to put their careers on hold. In some cases, many of the people who remained working, had to deliver extremely difficult news to impacted team members—news they never envisioned having to deliver. Having the chance to hear their perspective, too, helped me see things from their side of the fence, as it were. Or, to use the Indigo Bunting story, from the other side of the creek.

This concept applies to all interactions in the workplace, in a COVID world or not—at least it should. Several years ago, I worked with a gentleman who helped me see things from a different perspective when I was, let's say, a tad more cynical at the time than I am now, and certainly more than he was. We had just come out of a meeting where we spent the last 10 minutes listening to someone go on and on in such a way that left a sour taste in my mouth. He, to me anyway, came across as a little cocky and self-absorbed in the way he spoke about an initiative he was leading, and I said something to my colleague along the lines of, "Man, can you believe how much this guy thinks of himself?"

He then imparted the following words of wisdom on me that I can honestly say has changed the way I interact with colleagues to this day. He said, "Matt, in situations such as these, I always try to see it from their perspective and assume positive intent." I have now learned we oftentimes need to remove our own lens and personal feelings to hear and view someone else objectively and fairly without making false assumptions.

Regardless of the circumstance, everyone we meet in life brings a unique perspective to the table in every situation. The grumpy cashier we encounter at the grocery store may be finishing a 12-hour shift before heading home to take care of a sick loved one. The rude guy who honked his horn at a red light when we sat there for two seconds after it turned green, then sped around us like he was playing *Mario Kart*, may be rushing to the hospital to see a relative. The "annoying" telemarketer we just hung up on may be working in that job to put food on the table and perhaps earns his salary based, not necessarily on "booked business," but by at least being able to make his pitch before he feels humiliated because he can't even get "hello, my name is…" out, before we cut him off to tell him now is not a good time.

In the fast-paced world that I have referenced throughout the book, if there is one priority that we shouldn't allow ourselves to compromise on, it is this concept of taking the time to understand the perspective of others before we rush to judgment, and here is the birding story that helped make this concept come to light for me.

The Northern Mockingbird is not only the state bird of Florida, but one of the most common species I observed last summer. The picture used for the title page of this chapter was taken in my own backyard, literally. Not in the proverbial sense. Over the summer, I posted on one of the Facebook groups I belong to, just for fun, the following question: "What is the most common bird you see in your own backyard and what bird would you love to see as often but don't (and likely never will)? For example, I'd love to see (Blank) as often as I see (Blank). For me, I'd love to see Painted Buntings as often as I see Northern Mockingbirds.

As suspected, it was fun to see what people had to say. Many, like me, said the Painted Bunting. But what stood out the most was the number of people who shared that what they'd love to see more of, was the same exact bird I said I see often, almost too often. Yes, the Northern Mockingbird.

This made me pause. Because it helped provide this important reminder that we don't remember to be mindful of enough—perspective. What I considered to be "common," "no big deal," "nothing special," and something that isn't worth stopping to take a picture of, when dozens are in front of me at Plantation Preserve or my own yard, is the same species that others, many others, would consider themselves fortunate to be able to see as often. I cover some of this concept in more detail in a future chapter, but this change of perspective is what led me away from the "Oh, it's just an Anhinga" or, "Oh, look, it's just another White Ibis" mindset and helped me better appreciate every bird I saw, every time I saw it. You'll see more in the chapter on appreciation, but it all started with seeing things from the perspective of others. In this case, from a total stranger, and that's the point.

We think we do a good job seeing the perspective of our spouse, our kids, our loved ones, and friends but we don't always. It's why I said last chapter I would give Kristie somewhat of a hard time when she didn't like me being on my phone while we watched a television show together. I was looking at it from one perspective though—mine, not hers.

One thing to add about the Northern Mockingbird is that my mother, who, as I've shared before, lives about three miles from me, doesn't get any in her own backyard either, at least not that she's observed. While she lives on the water, with her yard backing up to a lake and thus enjoys seeing her share of herons and Wood Storks, the mockingbird had eluded her as well. Funny enough, the morning I shared a draft of this chapter for my mother to read—because I sent them one-by-one along the way—she texted me a photo she took at a shopping center a half-mile from her house and asked, "What are these guys?"

"What do you think?" I sent back with a smile emoji—yes, I use them too but not on the same level as my mom who has reached a Scholes-ian level with regard to her emoji game. In any case, yes, you guessed it, they were Northern Mockingbirds.

As it relates to the White Ibis, when I told you about the "research" during the trip to Delaware, this included joining a similar Facebook group for birdwatchers in that area. I stayed a member even after I left town, primarily because it included the state of Maryland, my home state as a reminder, so I thought it would be fun to stay connected to the "bird scene" there, too. One day, several weeks after I returned home, I stumbled upon a post from someone in that group who was so excited to share their rare and first-ever photo of a…White Ibis. The same species that, as I pointed out in chapter 6 when talking about the Glossy Ibis, I once saw 400 of sitting in a few trees together. Again, perspective.

I have said before that I wouldn't go as far as to consider myself grateful for some of the challenges I've had to overcome, along with so many others, during the spring and summer of 2020 but I have said several times, I am appreciative of them, because the challenges allowed me to, for the first time in such a glaring way, take the time to consider and understand other people's perspectives. Throughout the time spent out of work, I never truly worried about my financial security in such a way that so many others did. This understood perspective shared by thousands if not hundreds of thousands, made me look at almost everything I did during that time so much differently than I potentially would have been able to. It made me a better writer, for one.

I referenced the blog series I wrote that seemed to garner the admiration and appreciation from so many. I think, if I ask myself why that is, it's because I was able to capture the perspective of others besides just my own. Every time I wrote something—to borrow the cliché I used last chapter—I asked myself, "Does this pass the sniff test?" Could someone read this and think, "Man, that guy doesn't have a clue." I won't saying I always got it right, but I can tell you, I sure as heck tried.

I don't think it's necessary to get into the details here, but I'll also share, given the—I guess you could say—second major headline of 2020, the civil unrest and racial tension that seems to be plaguing our society as much as ever, that I did take the time, and I know I am not alone, to step back and listen in an attempt to understand a perspective that I've never experienced and never will—being a person of color in America.

The details of some of these conversations I had with friends and former bosses—people of color and people I am close with and have always enjoyed conversing with—as well as articles and blogs that I read to continue to try and learn, are somewhat irrelevant. It is more a matter of being able to acknowledge that, just because I do not share your perspective, simply because we don't share the same skin color, it doesn't mean that I cannot take it upon myself to listen, learn, and try to understand it. and just as importantly, respect it.

This lesson could never be as timely as it is right now. Public health concerns, race relations, social and environmental issues, economic insecurities, political views (lots and lots of political views), all of which have led to a polarization in our country that, for one reason or another, seems to be at an all-time high. Having everyone in the country agree on every issue is not the suggestion. I hope there is no one reading this thinking that I have this utopian view based on the positive outlook I've held on to these last few months which I've allowed to cloud my sense of reality. I wouldn't even find that to be a good thing. Disagreement and multiple perspectives are not only expected but necessary for a society, organization, and even family to thrive.

I do not think it is too far-fetched to suggest that taking a more direct and deliberate approach to better understand the perspectives of others on a given topic, would result in a more compassionate and empathetic society in general.

Much like my initial conversations when I first went back to work, giving people the courtesy of listening to their perspective, and then allowing yourself to be open-minded enough to truly digest it, allows you to develop a better understanding of where someone else is coming from, enables you to build more trusting relationships, and, ultimately, may help you to approach the way you live and work and parent just a little bit differently as a result.

Going back to the Birds of Paradise, which is where the two lessons on perspective intersect, sometimes to do this, you do in fact have to try, to the extent it is possible, to physically see things from someone else's perspective. In this case, another specie's perspective—the female Parotia. So, sometimes, you do need to put yourself in another person's shoes. Again, not with the goal of changing your own perspective but by gaining a deeper and greater understanding of theirs.

To crouch down to see their blocked view of the fireworks, and, maybe, to lift them higher. Not so their perspective is higher than that of your own. But to the point where they are at least even. So, they don't feel beneath you.

This concept can reap an unlimited number of rewards and benefits in all phases of your life, many of which we've discussed in the previous pages. The green employee who comes into your office with a question you may find remedial. The kid who shares his favorite topics with you and you can't fathom why they care so much. The spouse who wants you to understand why watching television together is not an occasion where multitasking is appreciated. The parent, brother, sister, or friend who wouldn't handle something the exact same way you might, but nevertheless, shouldn't have to either and shouldn't be made to feel judged or scrutinized because of it. In every relationship, it matters.

I think the other important thing to call out is that a different perspective doesn't mean it is a wrong one. I think this is to be assumed but, then again, far too many arguments are based on this notion, and, as I said, we are seeing it play out in unprecedented ways. When I said earlier that sometimes I don't have the right perspective when trying to photograph a specific bird, I'll clarify that sometimes I don't have the right perspective to see it and photograph it *clearly*, and in a way that yields the results I want. To see it better, I'd have to be willing to change my perspective but perspectives, like opinions, cannot be wrong by definition. However, if you think yours hinders your ability to see something clearly, then, just like in the physical sense, consider changing it.

In the most practical sense, I'll share an example of how different doesn't mean wrong. A few years ago, I was driving the family to a movie theater about 10 minutes from the house. As spouses sometimes do—both husbands and wives I'm sure are guilty of this—Kristie said to me, as I went straight at an intersection instead of turning left, "You're going the wrong way."

To which I replied, calmly of course, "No, I am going a different way. It doesn't mean it's the wrong way. Both ways will get us to the same theater at essentially the same time, where we will then see the same movie, and, most importantly, inhale the same obscene amounts of popcorn." Kristie doesn't love this example, but I share it because it is a textbook one when it comes to acknowledging someone else's perspective. In this case, it's a benign topic—directions but the principle applies regardless, and, in case you are wondering, we've since timed it, and depending on how you hit the traffic lights, it takes about the same amount of time to get to the theater from either of the two chosen routes. So, in this case, there really was no right or wrong, which is why I chose to use this example.

If "my" way took 20 minutes when hers took five, there's an argument to be made about holding on to a belief or perspective out of stubbornness or, worse, ignorance. It also needs to be stated that, just like Daniel catching the fly in the last chapter, there are exceptions to every rule. People who insist it's their "perspective," to justify their intolerance or hate, is a prime example. Racism, sexism, and the like are never "right" no matter how much someone feels entitled to their perspective. An exception to the rule, and in this case, an ugly one. But let's move on.

The last thing I'll note before I wrap up this lesson is this: taking the time to listen to the perspective of others should not be perceived as a sign of weakness either. Or, more accurately, that you are not someone who is strong enough in your convictions. Again, I assure you, this isn't the way to view this lesson. Rather the opposite. Showing someone that you are willing to hear them out, while still respectfully holding true to your own beliefs at the same time, makes you seem even more secure and "stronger." It shows that your beliefs are not simply based on your lack of knowledge on a particular subject and that you only view the world by taking just your own view of it into consideration. This is actually what makes someone, or at least their opinions, seem fairly weak—for the simple fact that they are one-sided.

So, the next time that you stumble upon a Northern Mockingbird and think, it's *just* another mockingbird. Remember that to someone else, seeing that same bird would be an absolute blessing. It won't make that mockingbird any less common for you than it already is, but you may just see that mockingbird with a little more gratitude than you did before.

Chapter 10

PUSHING YOUR BOUNDARIES AND PURSUING EXCELLENCE: THE PRAIRIE WARBLER AND THE PAINTED BUNTING

"I can never resist a chance for a better or different shot."
—A Facebook Birder

The Prairie Warbler taken at Plantation Preserve, September 2020 in Plantation, Florida.

In the last chapter, I hinted at this being a future lesson. Throughout the last few months, it's safe to assume that every time I went birding with the intent on taking photos of different and—with hope—new species, that I was at the same time, practicing every step of the way, and pushing myself to get better.

A few weeks ago, I came across yet another interesting post on one of the Florida birding Facebook groups from a gentleman who stated, "I have seen and photographed so many Prairie Warblers over the past few days but can never resist a chance for a better or different shot."

This comment not only gets at this concept of practice, continuous improvement, and the desire to pursue excellence in a chosen field or craft, it also touches on the focus of last chapter as well with regard to his use of the term "different shot." I can relate to it, not only in terms of my own experience with, ironically, the exact same species but with something else that I've talked about a lot already too—Disney. You are aware that going to Walt Disney World with my family was among my biggest hobbies and passions prior to COVID-19. My love of taking pictures there hasn't been touched on but Kristie has asked me, on many occasions, as I would make the family wait just a few minutes while I snapped away, "How many pictures of Cinderella Castle do you need?" Never enough, would be my response.

Fast forward to today and, like the gentleman in the above Facebook post, swap out the words "Cinderella Castle" with "Prairie Warbler." The Prairie Warbler is not only the warbler species I've seen the most of during my first experience with fall migration, it was, coincidentally, the first one I saw, too. On an early morning walk with my mom on a Sunday in mid-August, we passed a woman walking in the opposite direction who was excited to share as she walked by, "There's a Prairie Warbler and a Blue-gray Gnatcatcher just over that bridge."

"Cool, thanks," I said back as I admitted to my mom that I didn't know what either of those two were just yet. While that was the day that I did see and photograph for the first time, a Blue-gray Gnatcatcher—the same species that I highlighted throughout chapter 8—I did not have the same chance with the Prairie Warbler. Again, not necessarily knowing what I was looking for at the time, and not even aware that fall migration had begun, I hadn't prepared myself to be on the lookout for anything new. Yet another carryover lesson on preparation. I did see something yellowish flutter by at one point, but it wasn't anything I could identify.

By the end of that same week, I saw at least a half dozen at both the Plantation Preserve as well as the Plantation Botanical Garden. I haven't brought up this little park yet but it's another one to add to the list of undiscovered hidden gems that were right up the road. What I like about the Botanical Garden is that it is much smaller and thus a tad less intimidating than the Preserve that was about two miles away.

The Linear Trail isn't a tough hike, at all, but it is a long one. The Prairie Warbler, for example, that was on the other side of the bridge, as the woman we passed pointed out, is toward the end of the trail and about a mile away from the entrance. This is where, I've come to discover, most of the fall migrants can be found. So, going back to the days where I would only have 10 minutes or so to see "something new," this would prove nearly impossible today if I were to go the Preserve exclusively for those "quick hitters."

The Botanical Garden then, situated right next to the Plantation Historical Museum in what is considered the city's historic district, is a much more conducive park to visit if you find yourself with limited amounts of time. While you will not see as wide a variety of species there as you will at the Preserve, you can see plenty of them—the Prairie Warbler, for one. It was here, about two or three days after that Sunday walk with my mom, where I saw and photographed my first.

That first photograph wasn't great. It didn't turn out to be a Gray and Grainy Warbler, much like the Gray and Grainy Bunting from the previous chapter, but the Prairie Warbler's bright, almost blinding yellow color did not come through in the photos I took that day. That's fine, as I would see one several more times over the next few days, and even more as the month of August transitioned into September, which meant more of them had arrived. Each of these photos turned out to be better than the last but, again, like the gentleman noted, I never resisted the urge for more and better and different.

Here are a few examples for illustrative purposes and to help emphasize the point, and, going back to one of the first lessons in this book, a reason why I am fortunate to have not started my birding endeavors with this particular bird. I may have given up. I am glad I didn't.

This picture is the first one I took of the Prairie Warbler in mid-to-late August. Again, not exactly the fictional Gray and Grainy Warbler I sarcastically referred to above but, certainly, the  photo did not capture the bold yellow that defines this bird. The conditions were not great to begin with, and, because this was the first one that I'd attempt to photograph, the settings used didn't get it done, nor did the editing programs used after. Still, it was a milestone because it was my first confirmed sighting of the Prairie Warbler.

Attempt No. 2 would take place later that same week. (Note, I took several during attempt No. 1, but I consider each new sighting one attempt regardless of how many pictures are taken during

each). Also, at the Botanical Garden and, better, much better, I think. Better light, which is also evidenced by the green leaves, too, and certainly a closer representation of the bird's bright yellow plumage but perhaps I played it a little wrong because the yellow still didn't pop.

Now, we're starting to get closer. This wasn't my third attempt, but as I recall, more likely my fifth or sixth a couple weeks later. Still, better. Much better. And the first "head-on" shot where the Prairie Warbler is looking directly at me, and, I must say, I love his facial expression, which appears to be a combination of "Oh, hello there," and, "Umm, can I help you?" The yellow is starting to pop and even the sharpness of the bird in the photo is improving.

Here are a few more shots from throughout the month of

September, including more photos from the same attempt as the one above, which is also from the same day as the photo used for the title page of this chapter.

Each of the three photos above, the last two being part of the same shoot as the photo used for the title page of this chapter, is better than the first few photo attempts that took place just weeks earlier. The last one I included to illustrate the point that, while sometimes we get lucky—as I've pointed out throughout these lessons—sometimes we don't. Just imagine if that one, measly, little [insert expletive] leaf didn't choose to randomly dangle right in front of him. Man, all I can say is, Mr. Tim Laman may have had a new colleague at National Geographic.

In all seriousness, the series of photos, including the first slightly grayed out attempt, all the way through the National-Geographic-worthy last photo above (save for that darn leaf of course), helps to reinforce the core lesson on the importance of practice and pushing yourself to do better. To pursue better. As I've discussed all along, this series also represents the previous lessons learned along the way, too—the need to have the perseverance to not give in, yet also the patience to know you don't have to rush either because there will be more opportunities.

It should be noted that I still do, and will continue to, take photos of the Prairie Warbler, including this one I took in early October, after I finished this chapter, but I had to come back and add this  one. How could I not? I will continue to take photos every time I see a Prairie Warbler, just the same as I will for all species I observe. For one, it's for the appreciation of what I am viewing but, secondly, and not any less importantly, it's for the continued pursuit of excellence.

How many more photos will that be? Well, to quote my friend Kenneth, another member of one of the Facebook groups I belong to, "Only the capacity of my camera's memory card will hold me in check." He said this after stating, "I must admit to sometimes overdoing it when I see a beautiful bird in good light."

I hear you, Kenneth. I do.

Some of the everyday life examples I've shared already

touch on this notion. Earlier, when I shared that I only asked Noah to learn a Billy Joel song after he had been playing for about a year and a half, I also said, even though I knew he could do it, I knew it would still be a challenge for him. I also said that this was a somewhat separate lesson. This, of course, is the lesson where that aspect of the fortieth birthday request comes into play. To reset the scene, Noah had just received incredibly positive scores on his Piano Guild audition, and had earned the praise of his teacher, and, yes, rightfully so, was feeling good about himself.

As is the case with many hobbies we pursue, two things can happen if we taste some early success and become "good" at something. One, as this chapter discusses, this success and confidence that comes with being "good" at something, will drive us to continue to improve. To push. To pursue. To practice. To become better than we were the day before. To ensure the photo of the Prairie Warbler from mid-September looks nothing like the one from mid-August.

The second likely outcome is the complete opposite—complacency. Ever heard the expression, "Resting on your laurels?" Here's some ancient Greek mythology history for you that would make my YiaYia and Papou proud to know I am sharing with you here. If you're not familiar with it, this means to be satisfied with our past accomplishments, and not feel the need to keep practicing or focusing on getting better. In ancient Greece, the laurel was a plant that was sacred to the god Apollo and he would give laurel wreaths to the winning athletes of the Pythian Games.

Often seen as a precursor to the Olympic Games, the Pythian games also took place every four years. Unless there was a global pandemic, in which case they were postponed to the following year. So, yes, the athletes who won, truly rested on their laurels as they basked in the glory of their victory.

While it is certainly great to take a moment to pause and celebrate accomplishments after each step of a longer journey (as I shared in the chapter on progression), there is a balance between celebrating small wins before you move on and continue to pursue excellence versus taking an indefinite break to pat yourself on the back and say to yourself, "That's good enough."

Sometimes, for children, we need to instill this concept into them a little more directly ourselves, because they may not be as inclined to do this on their own when they are younger. Noah, clearly, never said to himself, or anyone else for that matter, "I'm good enough." Still, he may not have understood, and he may still not understand, that pushing ourselves to always get better in an ever-lasting pursuit of excellence is one of the biggest factors in how successful we will be in life.

I've said in most of the chapters that the lesson I am writing about is "one of the most important" or "one of the biggest" or "among the most critical." I am not trying to be hyperbolic. They are *all* important. However, they aren't all important for the same reasons. Continuing to pursue excellence, no matter how good you are at something, or how much success you've experienced, either personally or professionally, is, arguably, the most critical lesson shared as it relates to attaining continued success.

It's why, as I said in the chapter on time, that after 15 major championships, and becoming the first athlete in the world to break the $1 Billion net worth barrier, Tiger Woods, to this day, still has a swing coach, and probably a team of them. It's also why he came back after multiple, and painfully difficult, back surgeries and other procedures to win the Masters in 2019. It is, in my opinion, among the most remarkable accomplishments in the history of sports.

So, Noah, like all my children, is learning this importance at a young age, and hopefully it's a lesson that will eventually become his own in time, just as it hopefully does for Emma and Dylan. Dylan, my baseball player, is a good one. He could be a great one. Lots of kids can be. Hundreds across our city can be. Thousands across our county, hundreds of thousands across the state, and, of course, millions and millions across the country can become great baseball players.

I tried to explain this to Dylan in much that same way last year after he, like so many others do—the millions across the country—expressed interest in playing professional baseball. The lesson was not delivered in a discouraging way, like, "Yeah, good luck with that. What do you want for breakfast?"

No, it was framed the same way I framed this lesson and the Prairie Warbler. It's about the constant and ever-present desire and need to get better. To want to get better, too. It's about pushing yourself even when you think you've reached "good enough." I tried to explain to him that if he didn't want to get better, then someone else will but this is a lesson I didn't have to teach him alone.

I mentioned that last spring Dylan, unfortunately, only played one baseball game before his season was postponed and eventually canceled. What makes it even more unfortunate for Dylan, and his teammates, is that one of the assistant coaches on the team, Kenny Cruz, played professional baseball and made it to the higher levels of the Minor Leagues. Kenny's son was on the team. My friend, Wayne, the team's head coach, drafted him because he was a good player but realized that it came with a side benefit and a big one—his pro-ball player pops. Even though Dylan's season was cut unfairly short, the several practices held before the season was halted were among the most effective and valuable that he's ever had.

A few sessions with Kenny, who delivered the same message to Dylan, only with much more credibility, will hopefully stick with Dylan and serve him well in any future pursuit, just like Noah learning a Billy Joel song at eight years old.

One day, after Dylan shared his dream to play baseball at the highest level, knowing Kenny had done so himself, Kenny asked him if he wanted to stick around after practice for some "soft toss," a common drill used in practice from little league to the Majors, where a coach is on one knee and faces the batter from a few feet away and with their bodies parallel to one another. And, as the name of the drill suggests, softly toss balls at the batter to hit into a net. This is one of the most effective ways to hone one's hand-eye coordination and forces a batter to keep their eye on the ball as it comes in—harkening back to the last chapter—from a different perspective.

It was late. Dylan was tired and sweaty and hungry. So, he said no, thanks. I am not sharing this story to pick on Dylan, let me state that up front. Not many 10-year-olds would take Kenny up on that offer after a long, grueling, two-hour, Kenny-run practice during an unseasonably hot spring afternoon in South Florida. I shared a passion Dylan possesses when it comes to sports, which includes a passion for winning but, again, what doesn't always come naturally to children—it doesn't always come naturally to many adults either, in fact—is the need to say "yes" to questions like that when every ounce of our body is saying "no," including our stomachs, and his had been empty since lunchtime.

The point is, Kenny then ribbed Dylan in a way that a father never could, but still did, with the positive intent of showing Dylan that saying yes to such a question, staying for an extra 15 minutes, and then doing that every practice over the course of your youth playing days, for the next several years, can make the difference between you and anyone else dreaming to be baseball players. Dylan stayed that day, and the following practice, before Kenny had a chance to ask, Dylan ask him, "Coach, can we do some soft toss?"

Before the first game and, again, the last one too, there was a league-wide parade held as part of the opening day ceremonies but, as is the case every year, it didn't start on time. So, we had about an hour to kill where every parent stood around murmuring things under their breath, while nearly every kid across the league from all age groups, goofed around and played tag. Dylan noticed Kenny standing near the bleachers on the opposite side of the field, walked over to him, and asked if he wanted to play catch.

I was proud because I saw this as an early indication that Dylan was beginning to grasp the importance of this concept of practicing every chance you can get and taking advantage of every opportunity to get better. He didn't ask another player to play catch, though maybe he tried first. Either way, he chose someone who could push him and help him get better. Unfortunately, he only had one more practice after that opening game when the season was cut short. But, when baseball resumes, I know Dylan will be ready to continue the lessons learned last spring.

Let me also say that Dylan making the Major Leagues is not my goal for teaching him this lesson. Again, my positive outlook hasn't clouded my sense of reality. I've already discussed some fathers I know who let their own passion, and maybe their own dreams, trickle down to their children. That is not the case here. I want him to push and pursue and practice so he can become the best player he can become, whether he stops playing after youth ball or pursues it as a sport in high school or, perhaps, with continued practice and perseverance, college and beyond.

One of the greatest examples of this type of commitment to continuous improvement is Kobe Bryant, whose death on January 26, 2020, sent shockwaves through the world, well beyond the confines of sports and, to this day, hasn't completely settled. There is no debate that on the court his passion and drive is among the most admirable in the history of sports.

Kobe's death has left an indelible mark on many of us for several reasons, not the least of which was the sudden and tragic circumstances that claimed his life along with eight others, including his 13-year-old daughter, Gianna. Given the timing, it also seemed to come right at the onset of the pandemic, and, in hindsight, almost feels like the day the world changed.

It's safe to say, not only has the world changed since January 26, 2020, but the world has changed us, too. Many of us have had to say goodbye to the past, including parting ways with careers, colleagues, and the companies we've called home forever. No matter what hardships we face in our lives, we can take a page from Kobe's book, *Mamba Mentality*, which could be described as the relentless drive he possessed. It was also a term he coined that not only made him famous but led him to win five NBA championships and retire as one of the most accomplished and celebrated basketball players in history. In his own words, the Mamba Mentality means, "To constantly try to be the best version of yourself. It's a constant quest to try to be better today than you were yesterday."

The Mamba Mentality reminds us that only we can choose how we face the future by prioritizing our goals and going after them without fear, honing our craft, and having the commitment to not only win, but dominate. It starts with having the confidence and resolve to believe in yourself, first and foremost, or as CBS sportswriter, James Herbert, says, having a "foundation of unwavering self-belief." It's an empowering thought. No matter what happened to us yesterday, or what happens today, we should wake up tomorrow knowing that none of it should dampen our inner fire. The Mamba that lives inside each of us is there to guide us during times of adversity as well as triumph.

Since sports stories always lend themselves to this type of lesson, I'll share some more from that world. As stated, my older brother, John, is a college football coach. Earlier in his career, while serving as an intern on the defensive staff, he had the opportunity to coach under Nick Saban at Louisiana State University, better known by its acronym, LSU. This would be the coaching equivalent of learning how to cook by being an intern at Thomas Keller's The French Laundry or learning how to become an entrepreneur by interning for Jeff Bezos.

Love him or hate him, and many in South Florida do indeed hate him, based on his short stint with the Miami Dolphins after he left LSU following my brother's first season there, Saban is still unquestionably one of the most successful college football coaches in history. He is known for, perhaps, above all else, his relentless pursuit of excellence, which has enabled his teams to win seven National Championships over the last 18 years, including LSU in 2003 before my brother arrived, and as recently as this past January (2021) at Alabama.

In 2012, Saban and his Alabama Crimson Tide had just won the SEC Conference Championship, one of now 10 conference titles his teams have earned to go along with the seven national titles, after defeating the Georgia Bulldogs, 32-28. As he was standing on the podium waiting for the post-game trophy ceremony to begin, in front of thousands of spectators cheering, with confetti streaming from the rafters, the five-time SEC Coach of the Year took out a notepad and a pen and started jotting down notes in the middle of the mad frenzy.

Dan Wetzel for Yahoo Sports wrote an article about this. When Wetzel asked him about it during the press conference, Saban told him he was writing "field notes," things he wanted to improve upon for next game. Perhaps the four-point margin was a little too close for comfort but, if you're thinking this is a tad extreme, you wouldn't be wrong. Saban himself admitted as much when the question came to him. Regardless, if you want to know what the antithesis of what resting on one's laurels looks like, this is it.

"We won a championship, they haven't even given us the trophy yet, and I'm already thinking about what's next, what do we have to do next," Saban said. The only thing that makes this not that absurd is with that win, Saban had earned yet another berth in the National Championship game, and it's to be presumed that this reality first occurred to him before the champagne was even popped to celebrate the conference title. There's never a bad time to continue the pursuit of excellence, I guess. And, you can say it worked. The Crimson Tide went on to beat Notre Dame one month later in one of the most lopsided title games in recent memory, 42-14.

Oh, in case you were thinking that it's too bad John got to LSU one year after the Tigers won a National Championship under Saban, I am happy to share that John, who could write a book on perseverance the way that I wrote one chapter on it, would win one four years later in his final year at LSU before he took a bigger role at the University of Nebraska. The 2007 LSU team defeated the Ohio State Buckeyes, 37-24. As my parents and I cheered from the seats, John was on the sidelines, and then got to experience something few coaches, in any sport, will be able to—win a National Championship. He should write a book one day, with a ghostwriter, of course, and I know who can help him.

This leads to somewhat of a sub-lesson or theme that I noted in the title, which is pushing your boundaries. Sometimes, to do this requires a boldness that pushes you to not only want to get better but, also, to think you're always capable of getting better as well. It's almost a heightened state of confidence with an added kick of knowing that if you set your sights on a goal, and you practice enough, and push yourself enough to achieve it, that when the time comes, you will. John has had this. When he told the family that he wanted to be a college football coach the day after he graduated from Virginia Tech with a degree in business in 2001, everyone kind of thought he was a little bit nutty. Everyone but one person, himself. It is not only a continued pursuit of excellence that powers us to succeed, it is the bold belief it takes to know that we will, even if others express doubts.

My stepdad, Rick, who I've talked about throughout this book, has a favorite quote he likes to use which is, "Fortune favors the bold." When you push yourself to succeed, and keep getting better, you'll find that by putting yourself out there, even when others might call it risky or even foolish, the rewards can be plentiful. Rewards that wouldn't come to you if you're observing from the sidelines of life.

On the way to Delaware from Tallahassee, once I resigned myself to the fact that I was not going to drive 17 hours straight with three kids, I figured out a couple places to stop and stretch our legs along the way, as well as where we would stay the night. I should note, the drive to Tallahassee didn't save us a ton of time—four or five hours. Given it is on the western part of the state, in what is referred to as the panhandle, we had to cut back and head east before driving north to see my dad. Still, we did it because I knew it'd be fun to see my brother, and for the kids to see their cousins, and we had the time. One of the places I identified for the drive up was in South Carolina, just a few miles off the exit. It coincidentally happened to be a wildlife refuge, and one of the more popular ones in the state at that.

Okay, there was nothing coincidental about it, but I was driving, I was the adult, and, I decided, since we're stopping anyway to walk around for a bit, we might as well see some birds. Also, a quick search on eBird revealed that Painted Buntings—yes, the highly coveted rainbow-colored bird from earlier—could be found here, which truth be told, also was not coincidental. Around the time I had the revelation that Delaware would provide some unique birding opportunities, I also realized it meant the drive there would, too. After a little research, I learned that when Painted Buntings flew north in the winter, they wouldn't fly far. Many make South Carolina their summer homes, and this refuge, in particular, was a popular spot. The kids actually were fine with it and enjoyed being able to run around for a bit after sitting in a car for several hours.

As is often the case, luck played a part. We saw one Painted Bunting high in a tree. I snapped a few pictures, headed toward the car, feeling like, "Well, that was easy." We were in and out in about 25 minutes which made for the perfect pit stop as we continued north. I processed the photos at

the hotel later that night when we stopped in North Carolina, and much like the case with the Prairie Warbler, they were not quite good enough. Still, I wasn't disappointed. I saw a Painted Bunting, another "lifer" and, again, one of the most sought-after birds. One that, once I saw it on the cover of my mom's book, I said, "Wow, is that even real," and I saw it during a memorable summer road trip with my three kids. But I knew it wasn't good enough to be the center of my portfolio, let's put it that way, so I thought, "Guess I'll wait until fall."

As we headed back toward Florida about eight days later, after a great week in Delaware, the Painted Bunting reinserted itself in the corner of my mind. It crept up until it was front and center. I couldn't stop in the same place as I did on the way up for timing reasons but maybe I could figure something out. While getting gas and browsing on my phone, I decided that— and this pushes the term bold while in the middle of a 22-hour drive home with three kids after being gone for two weeks— maybe we could give it one more shot. Thanks to eBird again, I knew some had recently been spotted in Jekyll Island, Georgia, which is about a 20-minute detour off I-95 and only about 45 minutes from where we were at the time.

I figured during a 22-hour drive, an extra hour or so really wasn't going to make or break anything, so why not? I was driving, the kids were fine, and, again, when will I be on a road trip like this any time soon? I wouldn't. So, I turned off the exit and whispered to myself, "Fortune favors the bold, right, Matt?"

Unbeknownst to me before I arrived, Jekyll Island is huge, but it didn't take me long to discover that fact within minutes of pulling into gates. It's essentially a mini city, not a park. So, we  drove around a bit, and, honestly, even if I didn't see the Painted Bunting, it would've been okay. It was a beautiful area to check out and I was savoring the last minutes of this special trip, much in the same way I was savoring the last few minutes of winter break 30 years earlier. As I was pulling out of the campground area after no sightings, I randomly passed a sign that said, "Bird Sanctuary," and I turned left on a dime. Again, with a little luck on my side or, to use Rick's terminology, the fortune that would be the reward for my boldness, appeared.

I took about half dozen photos of the Painted Bunting, and I didn't need to look in my camera's preview screen to know they'd be good, but I still want more. And better. While as I type this, I haven't seen one here, yet with migration they have been sighted a lot, including by a new friend of mine, Ted. I'll speak more about him in the next chapter.

Maybe boldness runs in the family. My younger brother, Drew, has also had a propensity for it. His boldness goes back to his elementary school days, back when I was a young and somewhat fiery teenager. One evening, his boldness was on display for dozens of unsuspecting parents at Jones Lane Elementary School that night who were there that night and filming the end-of-year concert for the ages, featuring the most talented 11- and 12-year-old musicians the school had to offer. Mostly. We sat there with pride that day, as Drew was one of a select few pulling double duty. He sang with the chorus and then, along with just about four or five others, stayed on stage as part of the evening's headlining act: the school band.

While we were a little sad and perhaps a tad angry his name was omitted from that section of the concert program, we smiled with pride as he tried his best to blow that trumpet as though he was Louis Armstrong. His efforts were not met with the same glee by his conductor, who shot him glares with every missed note. The sadness had now evaporated completely, and anger had taken over. First, his name was left out of the program and now, an 11-year-old kid is receiving death stares for trying his best. Someone should tell this guy it isn't the New York Philharmonic after all, but maybe he had a passion for pursuing excellence, too.

Following the show, I decided to say something to the

leader of the band. "Listen here, sir. Help me understand how, one, you could leave a child's name out of a concert program when he has spent months practicing for this moment, and two, how could you give him those mean glares all night as if he *intentionally* sabotaged the performance? Please, I'll wait."

"Sir, your brother quit the band six months ago. Or so I would assume. He hasn't shown up since after winter break."

"Right. Got it. Carry on."

Boldness and perhaps someone who hated the end of winter break just a smidge more than me. Drew has never lived that down and I'll never let him. And now, neither will you. The reality is though, there is a lesson in this story which is why I chose it. Even though I find it hilarious 20-something years later that isn't the reason. It's to illustrate that boldness without preparation, practice, putting in time, and pursuing excellence, won't get you very far. On its own, it won't get you much of anything really, other than some dirty looks by elementary school band leaders.

It wouldn't take my baby brother long to figure this out by the way, which is why I can tease him about stuff like that. When I said some of my best memories of my youth were spent playing sports, it needs to be said that some of my best memories of young adulthood were spent watching him play them. Before I had kids, Drew was playing high school football at the same school I went to and was a great player on some great teams that had playoff success.

Drew pushed himself and pursued excellence for four years and during one of the most memorable games of his career, it paid off. In one of the most exciting games I've ever seen, on any level, Drew was named offensive player of the week for his performance lining up against one of the state's top defensive ends. He made this guy a non-factor, which is basically the most important job of what is often a thankless one: playing in the trenches on the offensive line. His team pulled out a come-from-behind win, after trailing 21-0, then again 28-7, before rallying in the final quarter to win, 35-28, against a team the school had never beaten before and, on top of that, a defending state champion.

Drew's worked hard to overcome a lot, just like many of us have, and has always done so with passion, and yes, a boldness but now one that is backed by those other things, too. When he moved to Southern California a few years ago, thousands of miles from family, he did so with that same inherent boldness but also driven by the pursuit of excellence and, eventually, the pursuit of something just as important. Soon after he moved there, he met his fiancé, Samantha. Depending on when you read this, she'll be my sister-in-law. But, as I write these words, their wedding is a few months away and will be held in the city of New Orleans. Perfect, the home of the jazz scene. Maybe this time, I'll play the trumpet.

To bring it back to sports one more before I put this one to bed, while Saban is regarded as one of the top college coaches of all time, Vince Lombardi is recognized as the greatest professional one. The Super Bowl Trophy was named after him, to emphasize my point. Lombardi once said, "Perfection is not attainable. But if we chase perfection, we can catch excellence." Everyone likes to use the phrase "practice makes perfect." I get it. It's catchy, it's cute, and it's an easy thing to say to the kids when they whine about another lesson or practice, but Lombardi had it right. We will never be perfect, but it shouldn't stop us from trying to be. It gives us a reason to keep pushing, to keep driving to get better. Or, to keep driving to see a Painted Bunting, but you get the point.

Just in case you're wondering about my daughter, Emma, let it be said, as I type this very sentence at 7:50 p.m. on Thursday, October 1, 2020, Kristie is giving me just a smidge of side eye. I am "pushing it" once again to be able to pick Emma up from gymnastics by 8:00 where, at six years old, she spends two hours every night of the week, and just to point out, she's never asked once if she could skip. If you want to talk about the pursuit of excellence, look no further. Also, it ain't cheap. I hope this book sells.

As I wrap up another lesson realizing, like all of them, I never truly wrap it up because it will continue to be a theme in the remaining few chapters, I'll close with this for now. Whether or not you aspire to be a winner on the national or world stage, such as Lombardi, Saban, or Tiger Woods, there is a universal lesson here—success is never final. It isn't final, which is why, after I go back and read, even after I've published one of my LinkedIn blogs, I have to resist the urge to make another edit or two. Sometimes I still will. Hopefully I won't need to with this book because I won't be able to, but I can always write another one.

I've mentioned before, my proud history working for Marriott. This slogan is one of the bedrocks of the company's history dating back 93 years. The current executive chairman of the company, J.W. Marriott, Jr., or Bill (but Mr. Marriott to those who work for him, or ever have) had a book published last year about his life and career leading what was once a nine-stool root beer stand in Washington, D.C., and is now the largest hotel company in the world. That doesn't just happen without a boldness and a constant pursuit of excellence. It's only fitting then that the 2019 biography written by Dale Van Atta shares its name, as that same familiar phrase that anyone who's ever worked for the company can say is a mantra exuded by every leader from Mr. Marriott down: *Success is Never Final.*

Indeed, it is not, Mr. Marriott. Indeed, it is not. Which is why I'll continue to take pictures of the Prairie Warbler every chance I get, and the Painted Bunting too, even if I need to push the boundaries to make those chances possible.

Chapter 11

PEERS, MENTORS, AND EXPERTS: THE SUMMER TANAGER

"FYI: That's a Summer Tanager"—A Birder Friend, Bruce

What Turned out to be a Summer Tanager taken at Plantation Botanical Garden, August 2020 in Plantation, Florida.

This is a chapter I feel like I've teased more than any other throughout this book. I didn't start out intentionally doing this, but I quickly realized as I was sharing some of the stories and lessons in the previous chapters—both bird-related and not— some of them would not make sense without the added context of including the important people in our lives that help teach us these lessons or help make one resonate a little more than it otherwise would have.

From National Championship-winning football coaches to piano teachers to former pro ball players turned little league coaches to birdwatchers we've never met in person but only on social media sites to 10-year-old nephews who teach us how to fish—much of what we accomplish in life, if not most of it, would not be possible without the influence, guidance, and tutelage of these key figures, who, as I shared earlier in the book and reinforce above, can come in all shapes and sizes, and can be found in some pretty unsuspecting places, too.

Still, this lesson and concept, of course, warrants its own separate chapter, even if this lesson has been a common thread in every previous one thus far. Think of those teasers I referred to in the opening sentence of this chapter as the movie trailer and this chapter is the actual movie. Because it cannot be overstated, if there is anyone out there who thinks they can do it all and learn it all, by themselves, then not only would I encourage that person to go back and re-read some of the stories in this book, I'd encourage them to close their eyes and think back to the person who taught them how to read in the first place.

I'll start with the photo on this chapter's title page, which, going back to the last chapter and the pursuit of excellence, is admittedly not my best. It wasn't chosen for the quality of the photograph but for the lesson it represents, and the reinforcement it provides to emphasize the overall theme of this chapter.

I mentioned earlier in this book, the first time I saw the Spot-breasted Oriole, after a week's worth of visits to Markham Park driven by perseverance, I soon discovered I'd see more of  them throughout the next few months. A couple weeks after I returned from Delaware, toward the end of July, I visited Markham Park again, and saw a juvenile Spot-breasted Oriole along with his family. I mentioned before that unlike the adults, which boast vibrant orange and black plumage, the younger ones have a pale yellowish color. This photo, on the right, is of that very same bird photographed July 29, 2020. And, to this day, among my favorite photos I've taken.

Later that same week, I paid my first visit to the place I introduced in the last chapter, Plantation Botanical Garden. I saw some great birds that first visit, including an adult Spot-breasted Oriole with its signature orange and black coloring. I enjoyed the park so much, I returned the following day and though I didn't see the adult Oriole again, I saw and photographed, and then uploaded to eBird, what I thought was another juvenile Spot-breasted Oriole—like the one pictured above that I had seen at another nearby park, Markham, just days earlier.

About two weeks later, I found myself, yet again, at the Botanical Garden, and on this visit, I bumped into someone whose name I recognized all over the Broward section of eBird, Steve. He has been among the most active, and one of the most helpful birders in the county. One of the most knowledgeable and passionate ones, too, I met Steve for the first time in person that day and we chatted briefly. He gave me some tips about the fall warblers that were starting to arrive, including the Prairie Warbler that I had already begun to photograph at that point, along with the Black-and-white Warbler that I showed a picture of in chapter 8. As we were parting that day, Steve said, "Oh, I think that photo you posted a couple weeks ago from here was actually a Summer Tanager."

This next part of the story, in all honesty, makes me seem

like the hypothetical person above who thinks they taught themselves how to read. "Nah, I am pretty sure it was a Spot-Breasted juvenile. I had just seen one like three days before it and I watched this bird fly from one tree to the next but, unfortunately, the only photo I took that was decent enough to share was the one from where it was right above me. Trust me. I am fairly confident it was a Spot-breasted Oriole. The picture might not be as convincing as it should be, but I saw it."

Okay, I don't know if those were my *exact* words, but that was pretty much the theme of the conversation. He offered some more insight into why he thought it was a Tanager, such as the shape of the beak, which now, after looking at them more closely, is different than the beak of the Oriole in the photo I had taken earlier that week. For whatever reason, I dismissed it, and never thought about it again.

That is, until I received a message on Facebook about two weeks later—in early September. If you recall me mentioning a person by the name of Bruce, who I inadvertently met up with in Coral Springs one day, this was that same gentleman. My initial encounter with Bruce in Coral Springs was also around the middle of August, about two weeks before he sent me the message that would be used, in part, as the title of this chapter, "FYI: That's a Summer Tanager on your eBird list from August 4 at Botanical Garden. I thought you'd want to know."

First, thanks, Bruce. Secondly, gulp. My apologies, Steve. We've since seen each other once or twice and I laugh about it now. Again, not an egregious mistake but perhaps a faux pas akin to some I've shared in this book—checking emails during a meeting, namely. In any case, yes, a lesson to be found here for sure.

A few additional notes here I'll share for some more color. One, this turned out to be the first confirmed sighting in all of Broward County of a Summer Tanager since fall migration started. I don't say this to brag, especially because it took me a month to learn this fact, but to share why it wouldn't have even been on my radar. Despite summer being in its name, the Summer Tanager is a fall migrant here. It was the first week of August, and, going back to the story last chapter and the woman who informed me about the Prairie Warbler at Plantation Preserve, I wasn't aware migration began that early. I was not on the look-out for a Summer Tanager, and, truth be told, wouldn't know what one looked like even if I were trying to find one.

Secondly, given I had just seen the Oriole of a similar color earlier that week, it was not a far-fetched conclusion for me to come to. None of this context excuses me from being a little, I guess you could say, overly confident in my bird identification capabilities, especially when compared to a gentleman who has been doing this for more years than I've lived in Florida.

I share that context to say, like the lessons from the previous chapter, just because we taste some initial success in a chosen hobby or craft, there is always someone who's a little more successful, a little more experienced, and knows just a little more. We shouldn't feel intimidated by this or even bad about it. I've been doing it for a few months. When I said earlier in the book that I was never afraid to ask questions of experts throughout my birding endeavors, this is true. I've shared numerous examples already and will share more in this dedicated chapter about mentors and peers but that doesn't mean, just like with many of the lessons I've written about already, there wasn't the occasional hiccup or two.

The thing to keep in mind here is, if that person who turns out to be a *little* better than us, a *little* more experienced than us, and *just a tad* (or, in this case, a lot) more knowledgeable than us on a given subject, and then voluntarily offers to help us learn something new or attempts to give us advice, we should probably take it.

That's not to say that we can't offer our perspective as to why we think something is what we thought. If our math teacher tells us 3+2 is 5, and we think it's 4, we shouldn't feel embarrassed about telling them why we came to that conclusion, especially if we felt confident about it. After they then explain that we're, umm, wrong, and, more importantly, *why* we're wrong, that's when we may need to allow ourselves to step down just a little bit from the pedestal we've placed ourselves on, and think, "Maybe I should listen to them."

That's how we learn. That's how we grow. The *why* is emphasized for a reason. Because knowing 3+2 is 5 without understanding why it is, won't do much good when we have to add 327+458. Learning the basic principles of addition is what allows us to move on to more complex equations. Anyone can memorize an answer as simple as a one-digit addition problem. If we don't take the added step of learning what makes the answer what it is, we won't be able to handle future problems that are more complicated and challenging later in life. In my personal example, knowing the difference in beak type from one species to the next is a more important takeaway than Steve, or anyone else for that matter, telling me what a certain bird is.

In fact, on the bird ID groups on Facebook that I've mentioned throughout the book, all of them come with an administrative rule that prohibits telling someone what bird they've unknowingly photographed without sharing why you've identified it as such. Oftentimes, the comment will be removed. Sounds tough but, again, it's all with an emphasis on teaching the "why." Saying, "Oh, that's a Great Egret," without saying, "Because of its large size, tall slender body with white plumage, black legs, and yellow beak" is not going to help this person as much as that additional information would.

This beautiful, and rare-for-that-time-of-year, Summer Tanager, even if not the best photo, turned out to be a wonderful surprise addition to my "lifer" list but, more importantly, it now serves as a terrific reminder of the importance of listening to, and accepting, the guidance and wisdom of those around us who—usually with the best intentions in mind—are there to help us get better. And forces us to remind ourselves, we don't know it all nor should we expect ourselves to, especially this early on in a relatively new endeavor. After two years, Noah will not be critiquing Billy Joel's compositions any time soon.

Speaking of piano, now is a good time to share another lesson about the importance of the people who help us in this never-ending quest for knowledge and growth. The skills we learn, and the confidence we gain while learning these skills, pay off and reap rewards in other parts of our life, in ways we may not realize. And, once again, we must thank our teachers and mentors for the critical role they played. Certainly, Noah deserves his share of the kudos for the story I am about to tell but Julie, his piano teacher, deserves her share too.

A few weeks into the school year back in mid-September, Noah's class had a "show and tell." In third grade, it's not something they had done yet and likely not something they will do very often. Noah's teacher wanted to make a Friday afternoon a little more fun than a Friday afternoon already is and decided to let the students show the class one or two personal items and then share why they meant so much to them (there's that "why" again). Plus, who doesn't love a little show and tell once in a while? Noah first asked Kristie and I, which we of course willingly gave him the permission to do, and then asked his teacher if he could play a song on the piano.

Noah not only played it—he nailed it. It was smoothest and most confidently he's ever played I *Just Can't Wait to be King* from Disney's *The Lion King*, a song he chose to learn last year that, of course, earned my immediate approval. I was very proud of his performance, not because of the strength of his playing but because of the courage he showed in wanting to. Again, a boldness, if you will, to put himself out there, even in a virtual setting, to play a musical instrument in front of 20 classmates and his teacher, and, presumably, siblings and parents who may have been listening with their child.

Yes, pride for my son first, and I'll resist the urge to drop a Pride Rock pun here, though it seems I didn't resist it well enough, was the first reaction. The second feeling that immediately came to mind was that of thankfulness. I sent Julie a message later that day and relayed the story, with my gratitude, and said, "It was your tutelage that has given him the confidence to be able to do that."

Julie wrote back with the following: "Oh, my goodness.

This message brought tears to my eyes and made my heart smile! I was just writing an email with some piano updates to share with my students and their parents, and I mentioned how piano helps in cognitive and motor function, self-esteem, confidence, etc. I am thrilled that Noah volunteered to play, and that he rocked it!"

I felt it was important to share the story with Julie for two reasons. One, I wanted her to know the impact her guidance has had on Noah, and the confidence he has gained because of it, and two, I wanted her to know how much we appreciated it. A similar thing happened with Emma's first grade teacher. If you recall, I shared a story earlier in the book about the confidence she seemed to have gained, literally overnight, following a couple of unexpected bumps in the road her first couple days of school. Expected for me, but not for a six-year-old who isn't used to these types of growing pains.

In any case, what I didn't say before was that the confidence she gained was not 100 percent attributed to her own sense of growth, nor was it solely attributed to my fatherly wisdom I shared with her after those first few days, nor was it Kristie's either. It was a group effort, with her teacher of course playing a significant role. Her patience, calm demeanor, and ability to instruct a group of six-year-old children—via video conference for six hours a day—is miraculous, and I took the time to tell her as much, as did many others, via the school's Facebook page, where all the school's teachers have been recognized by parents for continuing to educate our children in what is certainly a challenging teaching environment.

Emma's teacher's reaction was not unlike Julie's reaction but with one additional element I wanted to share. While all parents of young students were very much aware of some of the technology hurdles their children had to overcome those first few days, what wasn't as obvious was that many of the teachers were hurdling them as well. Teachers had to learn the same technology and not only learn it but feel confident enough in that technology to use it to instruct students.

So, Emma's teacher, who was experiencing some self-doubt herself during those first few days of the 2020 school year, then shared the following. "After reading those positive comments, it encourages me to continue to move forward, keep the faith, and know this is where I am supposed to be, even though I am going through some growing pains myself, which have made me more sensitive to the needs of my students and their families." There's not much I need to add here in terms of the importance of showing gratitude.

Taking the time to thank those who have provided valuable lessons to us should not be seen as a "nice to do" but, rather, a "must do." Oftentimes, these types of mentors, coaches, peers, or teachers come into our lives, teach us something, and then, in some cases, disappear forever. A baseball coach we had for only one season. A teacher who taught us for a semester. A birder we passed at a nature preserve and never saw again. I shared earlier, sometimes hobbies come into our lives for a season. Well, that phrase was borrowed, of course, as I shared, from the popular phrase about the people who come into our lives at various points. Regardless of how long they may have stayed in our lives, we should never miss an opportunity to thank them, to acknowledge their impact, and to ensure they know their guidance was not overlooked.

There may be some of these people where, at the time, we may not always understand and appreciate their methods but, with maturity and reflection, we learn to become thankful. I once had a high school football coach, Paul Foringer, who also coached my brothers, Drew and John, and coached state championship-winning basketball teams throughout his career in Montgomery County, Maryland.

Coach Foringer was, and still is, an old-school kind of guy. He's mellowed through the years, perhaps due to his own growth but likely also because some of the things one could get away with in 1995 would be a little frowned upon in 2020. He was a yeller. Not in an abusive way. He wouldn't cuss or even put a finger on your shoulder pad, but he'd get in your face from time to time and wasn't shy about letting you know when he sensed you were loafing, and if you were indeed loafing, he would *always* sense it.

He once said to me during my freshman year, in the fall of 1994, and repeated this to just about every one of his players over the last 40 or so years, "Don't worry when I yell at you. Worry when I stop. That's when I've given up. When I start to think you have nothing left to give. That you've reached your potential."

I didn't thank Coach Foringer for this while I was in high school. I didn't even thank him for it when Drew was hearing those same words nine years later. When I was living in Maryland and covering high school football games as a freelance writer, one of the teams I was fortunate to cover was my alma mater, Quince Orchard High School. So, 17 years later, in 2011, when I was covering the team on its way to a state title run, after I was already a father of two (with Dylan born in 2009 and Noah born during that season in 2011), it was then when I finally took the opportunity to thank him.

Every leader, boss, mentor, or teacher I ever had from that point on—following those hot and long August practices in the muddy fields of Quince Orchard High School in the mid-1990s—I looked at differently. While none of my bosses at work were "yellers," I came to understand that providing feedback on my work or offering simple guidance about email etiquette at the office, came from the same place Coach Foringer's words came from. They saw more in me—perhaps more than I saw in myself. They knew I was capable of more.

I started off this chapter by saying this lesson is not exclusive to the formal coaches or teachers we've had along the way but about the unsuspecting ones as well as the peers and friends who become part of our journey too.

Not unlike when I moved to Florida and really got immersed in the Walt Disney World photography scene, which then inspired me to join some groups and sites that allowed me to learn from others and engage with other "enthusiasts" like me. Well, when I dove headfirst into birding, I did the same. So, this chapter is also for them. Many of these peers and experts may stay "virtual" friends, especially in times like these with social distancing still top of mind. Nevertheless, whether I ever meet these people face to face or not, they helped me in my journey in one way or another.

Paul, the gentleman who was extraordinarily generous with his time when helping me successfully locate the Florida Scrub-Jay (and tried to help me locate a Red-headed Woodpecker). We've continued to correspond, and I'll share a story next chapter that relates to this lesson but I'm saving it for a reason.

Bruce, who, yes, not only helped convince me what I had

photographed in August was a Summer Tanager but has been great about sharing his wisdom with novices like me online. Thanks to him, I discovered another gem of a park—the one where I  bumped into him in Coral Springs and he let me tag along for a bit—Cypress Hammock. I've now been to this park a couple times. I've photographed several new species these last few months, such as the Pileated Woodpecker. Man, this bird is going to town on that wood like nobody's business.

Steve, yes, whose knowledge I took for granted, and won't again. Like Bruce, our three face-to-face encounters were by happenstance, and, despite the gaffe with the Tanager, I'll be honest, I've learned more in 10 minutes of conversation with Steve over a few different meetups than I've probably learned in the four or five books I've bought over the last several months.

There are dozens of others, if not more, who either took the time to answer a question or two, share some wisdom, compliment me on a photo I've taken, or just shared a cool photo of their own that inspired me to pursue new types of shots as well—all of them have been a big part of my overall experience these last few months.

Another I'll spend some time talking about is the gentleman I mentioned last chapter named, Ted. Truth be told, as I write this, Ted and I haven't met in person either, though he promises to invite me over soon to view his family of Painted Buntings that he has somehow already been able to attract, like some sort of Bunting Whisperer. Nevertheless, he lives a couple miles from me and sometime in August, when I was browsing through photos on Instagram that had been taken at Plantation Preserve, I noticed some of his shots. We sent a couple messages and then exchanged phone numbers.

Ted and I became fast friends even though we still have never seen each other face-to-face and there is a bit of an age difference. (He's semi-retired as he calls it, has a 38-year-old son who is a professional photographer, and has a grandchild, too). He came into my life around the middle of August, when I was still looking for work, school was getting ready to start, and I was just not feeling "it."

Ted and I had some good conversations—all via text, mind you—where we chatted about life, work, fishing (he's an avid fisherman too), the importance of family, and he gave me a ton of great advice about how I, too, could attract some Painted Buntings in my yard. The bird bath I am staring at as I type this was his suggestion. Of course, given that I still haven't seen any Painted Buntings, maybe the advice wasn't so great after all (I am only teasing, Ted). For whatever reason, Ted seemed to have entered my life to help lift my spirits at a time when I needed it, even though he didn't know I did.

I hope to meet Ted soon, and presumably will, before this book is even finished but I felt the need to mention him here because, again, in addition to the formal teachers and coaches we've all had at various points in our lives, it can also be chance encounters with strangers that turn out to basically be neighbors we didn't even know we had, that can help us in significant ways as well.

Of course, as I often do, I suppose I buried the lead here. I saved this for near the end of the chapter, though for a reason because, let's face it, I had plenty of opportunities to move it toward the top had I wanted to. In any case, even though this is not the beginning of the chapter, this section of the overall lesson is about the beginning. Each of our beginnings, and the people who worked their hardest to ensure all our dreams could come true.

Whether these were your parents (or just one of them who played the role of two), your grandparents (or just one of them who played the role of two), stepdads (but as Rick would say, bonus dads), bonus moms, aunts, uncles, older siblings—the kind who stick up for you even if you quit the band—or any combination in between, we must not miss the opportunities to thank our parents, or parental figures, while we can.

For those of you who no longer have this opportunity, I wish I had something poignant to offer but perhaps silence is more appropriate.

For those of us who do, though, don't squander the opportunity to thank them. Like right now. I want you to read my book, but it can wait. The phone call to a loved one you just realized—after reading this very sentence—you haven't spoken to in two months, cannot, and it shouldn't. Whether or not you're a parent yourself, or plan to be one day, aspire to be the kind that makes one of your kids want to drive 17 hours there and 22 hours back, with three kids of their own, to see you when they're 40 years old. Be the kind of parent who teaches your kids that living with a positive mindset and believing that good things are in store for them, even if they don't believe it themselves, can change their life in unimaginable ways.

After you make that phone call, which I assume you did because now you're back, I'd like to ask each of you reading this for a couple more favors. Yes, I know I am being greedy here but do this next. Think about someone else who has made an impact in your life—professionally, personally, or academically. A teacher, a boss, a coach, or even a best friend. If that person is still a part of your life in any capacity, and, frankly, even if they're not, consider taking the opportunity to let them know how much you appreciated them and the wisdom they shared, the lessons they taught, and the guidance they provided, even if it was years ago.

It's never too late to say, "Thank you." Remember, I was 31 years old before I thanked my high school football coach from my freshman year of high school, and, man, even at 40 I still have nightmares about the hill that we ran up and down when he felt some of us could use a little tougher of a lesson on loafing, Mount Foringer (don't ask).

Additionally, (yes, one final favor) think about how you could be that difference maker for someone, too. You don't have to be a formal teacher or coach or a parent to be able to lend some friendly advice to someone who could use it—a colleague, a neighbor, a novice at the hobby that you've been doing for years. I mentioned in a previous chapter that the way I was treated when I returned to work is what helped me find my footing so quickly after several months away. Be that person who can help someone find their footing.

Take a moment and reach out to a new colleague who may be wrapping up his first week and ask him how he's feeling. What you'll likely find, like Julie's reaction to the story I shared about Noah playing for his class, is the reward you get for helping, teaching, and inspiring others is as much of a reward as learning a complicated new piece of music you never thought possible.

With that, I'll close this chapter with a final thought that also ties back to that same story of Noah and his piano and the confidence that has now permeated throughout other parts of his life, namely school. If you are a parent, you already know there is nothing like seeing your child thriving and learning with confidence. That gift, which was delivered thanks to his teacher and her passion for music that was then taught to my son, is an infinitely greater gift to me than the Billy Joel song was last June, and that was pretty darn special, too.

To tie into that lesson, it's safe to say this book is the physical manifestation of what can happen to us when we become passionate about a new hobby. When we take the time to learn from others who help us improve, help us get better, help us pursue excellence, and keep wanting to learn more. As I have shared, after my first visit to Plantation Preserve on May 14, I didn't think that birding would ever lead to any of the growth and learning that would carry over into every aspect of my life ever since. And writing a book about it would have sounded absolutely ridiculous at the time.

It needs to be said that I certainly would not have learned as many lessons, ones that now fill the pages of this book, if it weren't for the generous advice and the friendly help of peers and experts, like those who take the time to point out that what we might think is a Spot-breasted Oriole, is actually a Summer Tanager.

Chapter 12

POSSIBILITIES: THE BLACK-BILLED CUCKOO, THE BLACK-WHISKERED VIREO, AND PROBABLY NOT A BAHAMA MOCKINGBIRD

"Dude, you got a Black-billed Cuckoo!"—A Birder Friend, Paul

This chapter's lesson, as we near the end of the book with just a couple lessons remaining, might actually be the one that can best answer the question that I've received the most these last several months: "Why birding?"

While the lessons I have shared in the previous chapters can certainly help answer that question with relative ease, the truth is that none of them, on their own at least, can answer the question as succinctly as this one individual lesson can. Because, even when I consider all the lessons I've learned; the cathartic visits to the places I've often referred to as my sanctuaries; the long walks alone spent lost in my own thoughts; the early morning walks with my mom that always seemed to lift my spirits; the adventures I had with my kids when we were on the prowl for new, fun, and undiscovered (by us, anyway) species; and the interesting things I read and the engaging discussions I had as I learned more and more along the way, none of these necessarily answer the question "why."

Before I answer that universal question, I need to go back to the beginning for a moment. I mentioned fairly early on in this book that, based on the number of interests I had and always have had, people gave me a hard time, all in good fun, when I first started getting into birdwatching and shared some of my favorite photos on my social media accounts. One day, a few weeks after I started doing this, I was chatting with an old friend of mine, and at one point in the call he asked what I had been up to that day. After I shared that I had just seen some cool new birds that I'd been wanting to see, he quipped back with, "You're still doing that? I thought you'd have moved on to something else by now."

Ha-ha-ha.

It didn't help that right around the time I started to share some of my bird photos, the *Washington Post* ran a story with the headline: "Amid the pandemic, people are paying more attention to tweets. And not the Twitter kind."

The May 22 article included the following quote from Mike Parr, President of the American Bird Conservancy, "There's a surge in interest in birdwatching right now. People are in their houses and running out of Netflix and Zoom meetings and wondering what to do and they're realizing there are birds in their backyards."

So, when I still get the occasional queries from friends of mine that I've known for years, some as far back as childhood, that all sort of hint at that same question—What is it? Why? Is it *that* fun? Sometimes, before I can even get my words out, they attempt to answer for me. "Ohhhhh, right. Yeah, I read something about that in the *Post* not too long ago. I get it. You're one of those people. So, how are the kids?"

Wait, let's back up. *Those* people? No, no, no. This is not some passing fad. I am not one of *those* people. Those people offend me. Actually, they don't. I don't even know them, and, in truth, maybe I *was* one of them. Maybe to the Bruces and Pauls and Steves of the world, I was some sort of Johnny-come-lately or Matt-come-lately but, even when the article first came out, I didn't feel like I was. And I especially do not now. Notice the date of the article: May 22. The day of my Northern Cardinal sighting: May 21.

This is why I felt that to answer this question I needed to go back, for just a moment, to the beginning of this book where I shared that Cardinal story. I ended that chapter by saying that was the day I was starting to "get it." I, of course, didn't know the impact it would have yet, but I knew a couple things to be true—that I was hooked and that this would be more than just a casual hobby. I could feel it, even if the "why" hadn't been crystalized at that point.

Because of this lack of crystallization, I guess you could say, I didn't know how to articulate any of it, or wasn't sure if I even could. If I think back to some of the times when I felt like I was "sneaking" a quick visit to the Preserve, this is perhaps the reason. Kristie didn't necessarily care if I felt the need to get out of the house for a few minutes and have some time to myself after taking care of the kids most of the day, but I suppose I thought that if she were to ever ask me what it was about birding, that even 10 minutes of it here and there drew me to it so much, I wouldn't even have been able to articulate it to her at that point in my journey. I didn't feel like anyone, frankly, could understand, at that point, just *what* it was. *Why* birding.

At this point, I am prepared to answer it. And I can do so with one word: Possibilities. I know what you're thinking: "That's it? That was the big reveal? That's just the title of the chapter." True, but it is the single best word to use to answer the question that I've received the most since I snapped my first picture of a Limpkin during my first visit to the Plantation Preserve Linear Trail. It's a lesson I learned that day, again without knowing it, it's one I've learned every day since, and it's one I'll learn every day for the rest of my life. And thus, why I'll repeat it again: Possibilities.

The second you get out of your car, you never know what you're going to see but once you step one foot on a trail, from that moment forward, the possibility always exists that you will find something special. Something rare. Something new. Something you never expected. Something you've never even heard of. Something that gives you reason to think anything's possible.

You may not always. It's happened to me plenty of times, especially in those 10-minute visits I referenced earlier in this chapter but plenty of times, it did. The fact of the matter is those visits are irrelevant. Regardless of how many times I did or didn't see something new or special, with every new adventure, every new park I checked off the list, every detour off I-95 during a two-week road trip, every 90-minute drive to Martin County, every time I drove past a tree in Immokalee and looked up, the possibility was there. It always was. It will always be.

When you find yourself, at times, looking for signs that there is a reason to remain optimistic, if you're not looking in the right places, you likely won't find many, if any, signs at all. In the chapter on perspective, I shared that, for a variety of reasons, I felt the country had reached a state of polarization the likes of which I'd never seen before in my lifetime. It is enough to make you bow your head and pray to whomever and whatever you need to, but this cannot be the way we want to be living as a society.

On top of that, I was in the midst of grappling with a lot of personal demons in a sense—the self-doubt, the self-defeat, the guilt for feeling those things when I knew I had so much for which to be grateful, even still. The guilt for squandering some of those quiet moments at home with the kids, where my mind would drift to some of these darker places. But it was also during some of the most challenging days of my unemployment, the days where I couldn't get out of my own head, the days where I beat myself up a little as I watched Kristie working hard in our home office as I scoured job boards trying not to feel dejected or deflated, the days where I felt like I needed something more to cling to. On those days I realized that not only was the possibility to experience something special and different the single most alluring aspect of this newly discovered passion and the answer to the "why," I also soon discovered that the lesson on possibilities was one that I probably needed most during those most trying days, too.

Because if I could be walking out of Plantation Preserve, headed to my car, and have a Cooper's Hawk, a bird I'd never seen before, swoosh by me in a flash, but then land five feet away and  allow me to take as many photos as I wanted, well, what other possibilities are out here? Out there? For me, for my kids, for my family? We never know. That's what makes it great. That's what gives us hope. That's what gives us reason to think "why not?" And that's what makes it my "why."

If I could be sitting at the resort pool, while on vacation with my family in Hilton Head, South Carolina, hear a strange call that compelled me to get up from my lounge chair and walk around the corner—with camera in hand, because I always had

it at that point—and see a
Bald Eagle 15 feet away in a
random pine tree, then what
else might be right around
the corner? What possibilities
exist even if I don't see them
from my current viewpoint?

What is out there for me that I don't know about but could
find out simply by getting up and away from my comfort zone?
Literally, because in this case, that lounge chair was amazing.

Which is also why it's important to not be discouraged
if you don't see something you sought out to—like the Red-
Headed Woodpecker. Because then you close yourself off to the
possibility of discovering something else you hadn't even thought
about, but beautiful just the same—including butterflies, flowers,
and sunsets. Sometimes, just being there, embracing nature is
enough, similar to my first experience at the Everglades when I
saw only a grasshopper.

Knowing that something special and unexpected could
happen when you weren't even looking was how some of my
most memorable stories started. I'll start with the one that
perhaps is most responsible for this chapter's discovery: the
Bahama Mockingbird (but probably not one).

By the end of June, I reached a point where my visits to

Plantation Preserve, at least in terms of the birding itself, were not doing it for me, I guess is the only way to put it. I won't say I saw everything I would be able to see there during the middle of summer, because again, there's always the possibility to at least see something new, but I had hit a bit of a slump in that regard. By then I was already venturing out to farther away places, but I was a little disappointed that the days of going to the Preserve and being almost guaranteed to find something new seemed to be a thing of the past. At least in the middle of summer. On one of these late June evenings, though, I learned the lesson that would change every future visit from that point forward—there or anywhere else.

It was one of those visits where not only had I not seen anything new, I hadn't seen anything. At all. As I was leaving the trail on my way out, I saw a bird all alone in a tree and something about it caught my eye and I snapped away. I got home, uploaded the photos, and thus the research began. As I used to do, and sometimes still will, to at least get me on the right track, I uploaded the images to one of the identification apps I had downloaded. These apps are not 100 percent reliable, but frankly, nothing is. I like to use them, especially then, to give me a starting point before I sought the opinion of others on Facebook. At the time, I wasn't a member of any of the Florida groups I now frequent the most, otherwise I'd have sent it to Bruce or Paul and see what they said first.

Back then, I didn't have the same "peers" as I do now, and so after uploading it to one of my apps, I was surprised to see it suggesting a Bahama Mockingbird. For two reasons. One, Florida is nice but it's *not* the Bahamas. And two, just what the heck is a Bahama Mockingbird?

After the app provided that suggestion, I did a little research on my own and I learned that the Bahama Mockingbird, a close relative of the species that I've mentioned a lot throughout this book—the Northern Mockingbird—can indeed be found in Florida. It's rare. It's uncommon. It's not expected but, it's possible.

Even in my earliest days I knew I wasn't going to trust the app alone, and even if I wasn't already using sites such as eBird to track my sightings—which I was at that point—I'd still of course want to know with certainty if I had seen and photographed something fairly rare, and at the time, something I didn't know existed. I shared the photo along with a brief explanation on one of the bird identification groups I belonged to at the time, again not specific to the state of Florida. I added this at the end of the post: "I know the odds are slim that this is a Bahama Mockingbird. So, if it's "just" a Northern Mockingbird...well, that's fine with me but, until I hear otherwise, I will assume I snagged a gem."

I'll also call out my intentional quotes around the word

"just" with regard to the Northern Mockingbird, yes, the same species I said I see almost *too* often—because even then, I wasn't going to be that dismissive of a common bird I'd see regularly, especially one that represents the state of Florida.

The debate among those more qualified to weigh-in began but one comment specifically is what served as my biggest takeaway from that experience. "Always assume you have the more common bird, then try to prove why it's not. You have a Northern Mockingbird there."

Now, in my earliest days, I didn't know if this was a "thing" or not in the birding community. I have come to understand why this is the best practice, and I'll share more in a moment why. Nevertheless, at that time in particular, his comment puzzled me, especially when you compare it with mine. "Until I hear otherwise, I will assume I snagged a gem" versus "always assume you have the more common bird."

While I have since come to understand that this is the preferred approach, which is because—going back to last chapter—one must prove the why beyond a reasonable doubt and I get that, even though it sounded like a negative way to approach bird identification. Now, with a few more months under my belt and more appreciation for those who take this stance—including Steve—I'll be honest when I say it still seems opposite to the positive nature in which I have tried to view this hobby in general. It almost takes a "guilty until proven innocent" position but, again, I do get it.

As it turned out, despite a few people being in my corner, most of the folks who commented that day felt strongly it was a Northern Mockingbird. Not *just* a Northern Mockingbird. But a Northern, nonetheless. And it probably was but it didn't matter. The thought that it *could* have been something much rarer was enough to reinforce this concept of possibility. Because there have been sightings of this bird in Florida—Paul, who I've talked about quite a bit, has seen a few over the years.

However, it gave me a renewed energy, especially about Plantation Preserve itself, which as I said started to feel a little on the stale side given the mid-summer state. From that day forward, whenever I went—there or anywhere else—I walked in and knew that something special could be out there.

I am sure other hobbies and activities provide this sense of possibility, but in honesty, not one of the many I have engaged in over the years does. Certainly not this sense of wonderment and a curiosity of the unknown. In fact, a few years ago, I appeared as a guest on a Disney podcast hosted by a gentleman who's since become a friend of mine, Brendan. His show is called "Detour to Neverland" and it features Disney enthusiasts, bloggers, Instagrammers, YouTubers, merchandise creators, etc. Brendan interviews people and asks questions about their passion for

Disney and invites them to share their stories. He always ends the show with a series of what he calls quick-fire questions and they're always the same. One of them is: "What's your favorite attraction at Walt Disney World?"

Most others gave many of the popular answers that anyone who has been to Disney would expect to hear: Space Mountain, Splash Mountain, Tower of Terror, and the like. My answer, which surprised Brendan since he hadn't heard it yet from a guest, was Kilimanjaro Safaris at Animal Kingdom.

"Interesting, Matt. Why?"

"Well, Brendan, it is the only ride or attraction at Walt Disney World, where no matter how many times you experience it, you are guaranteed for each time to be different."

I won't assume everyone reading this is familiar with this attraction. Here is the official description from the Disney website: "Explore the Harambe Wildlife Reserve, home to 34 species living in 110 acres of picturesque open plains, shady forest landscapes and rocky wetlands. Your rugged safari vehicle is driven by an expert guide, who helps point out animals and shares fascinating wildlife facts during this extraordinary 18-minute expedition."

This was the reason for my answer to Brendan. No other theme park ride provides that sense of wonderment I mentioned above. You are in an open-air vehicle, viewing and sighting real species in as natural of a habitat as it can be and without getting into the details, Disney has been meticulous about animal conservation, preservation, and ensuring these animals do not feel as though they are living in captivity. I've seen lions, mandrills, elephants (including a baby when it was first born in 2018), giraffes, hippos, and dozens of others but never the same groupings twice.

So, yes, I suppose any hobby that includes viewing wildlife provides this sense of the unknown. Birding, I think, provides it the best of all based on the sheer number of overall species one can try to observe over their life. Like Peter Kaestner who, if you recall, has seen more than 9,000. Myself, just a few months in, more than 100. A meager number compared to Kaestner, but going back to last chapter, this doesn't intimidate me but inspires me. I won't reach 9,000 but maybe 500 one day? Maybe 1,000? Who knows? It's possible, though, and that is the very point.

While I quickly got past the fact that what I saw that day in late June was not anything that unique, I kept that "anything is possible" mindset, and frankly sometimes I still do, with a bit of a naiveté. Toward the end of September, I was on a Sunday morning walk at—you guessed it—Plantation Preserve, with—right again—my mom.

This was about two weeks after I started back at work, and, because I was working, my birding endeavors went from four or five times a week, to once or twice. Which, by the way, is not such a bad thing. It makes those fewer occasions more special. On this particular morning, the walk was the perfect combination of leisurely, therapeutic stroll, and uplifting conversation, mixed with, as I said in a previous chapter, "Hush, mother I need to focus," said with nothing but the utmost respect, of course. We were in the back part of the trail, where most of the migrants can be found, to remind you of that note I made earlier in the book.

We were stumbling around an area known as the Indian Mound, and maybe because I had been away a week, I was rusty? Overwhelmed? Either way, that day I was Mr. Miyagi, *not* trying to catch three flies at once with a pair of chopsticks, I was trying to catch 10. I felt as though I was watching a ping-pong match, so I closed my eyes for a second and tried to drown out the distraction and told myself to focus—yet another example of the lessons carrying over from one to the next.

I resumed my search and saw several cool birds that morning—more Ovenbirds, some Northern thrush, a few different warblers and then, hmm, I don't know. "I think this is a Red-eyed Vireo, ma. I've seen one before but not from this close. It must be though, look at those red eyes. This is awesome."

I stood there that morning and took several shots of this would-be Red-eyed Vireo. We saw a couple more species and left the trail after another one of our great walks. We even bumped into Steve on the way out and I feel a little bad about it in hindsight and I'll explain why in a moment.

In fact, and I'll ask my mother to corroborate this story, this was the day Steve was telling us about a rare-for-Florida hummingbird that he thought he saw earlier in the week, a Rufous Hummingbird, but he was back with hopes to see it again, so he could prove that it was just that. "Otherwise, if you see a hummingbird in this part of Florida, it is a Ruby-throated," as he explained. That comment helped provide more clarity to the whole concept of assume common until you can prove rare. Again, not too proud to keep learning from those more knowledgeable.

Later that day, I uploaded my photos to my computer and clicked through, with the same sense of curiosity and wonderment that I had on May 14. I got to the suspected Red-eyed Vireo and it didn't look quite right for one. So, I uploaded the photo, not to an app but, this time, to a Florida-specific Facebook group, where some of my new buddies would be likely to weigh in.

No commentary. No preamble. Just: "Plantation, FL. Any help with ID?"

Within seconds, one of my peers did. Paul, the same gentleman who guided me to the Florida Scrub-Jay like he was a tech support operator helping me fix my computer.

"Dude, you got a Black-billed Cuckoo! Is this at PPLT?"

After I answered him back that yes, that was taken at PPLT—Plantation Preserve Linear Trail, I then thanked him for the ID help and, since we had corresponded a bunch in the past, I then sent him a direct message.

"Paul, help me out here. Is this *good?*"

At this point my post was already starting to generate a mix of "Wows" and "Holy cows" and the like. A few people, from other parts of the state, asked me where in Plantation this was. Some seemed willing to drive an hour or two away for a chance to see this bird, what I had thought was a regular fall migrant, the Red-eyed Vireo. Not *just* a Red-eyed Vireo, but nothing worth driving a couple hours to see, given their regularity.

Paul and many others told me that this was not a rare Florida migrant. It was *very* rare. Wow, I hit the jackpot it seemed but, unlike the Bahama Mockingbird incident, this is the case where I assumed that I did have a more regularly sighted fall migrant. In fact, my friend Ted

had shared with me earlier that week a great photo he took of one at the Botanical Garden.

The Black-billed Cuckoo wouldn't have been on my radar, given its scarcity in the state, any more than a Penguin would have been back in May. But more and more people started to chime in, and part of me started to feel guilty to find out that people who have been doing this for 10 years have never seen one of these, and then tell me what it is I've found with a big "Congrats," not a "You jerk, how unfair" (even if they *may be* thinking it, but likely aren't).

The Black-billed Cuckoo. A great reminder—a much better one than the non-Bahamian Bahama Mockingbird—of the power of possibility. A couple more points of color on this one before I share another example. I said last chapter when mentioning Paul and all the help he's given me that I had a story I was saving for this chapter and this is it. When I talk about finding coaches and advisors in unsuspecting places, this is another perfect example. The expert, Paul, that day—along with what I'd learn would be many others—learned from the beginner. This time, I was the one providing the step-by-step guidance for Paul.

Paul was happy to tell me, and I was happy to hear, the next day he went to the same place I had found the Black-billed Cuckoo, and after an hour or so of waiting—yes, he needed to exercise the same patience I've learned myself is often needed—to see what I stumbled upon just one day earlier. What's more, while there he ran into another long-time birder who I've seen at the Preserve but never spoken to because he always looks so serious. He had been there since sunrise, as Paul told me, and it took him five hours to see it. Wow. So many of the lessons wrapped into this one story of a Black-billed Cuckoo.

Just remember this—when the 22-year-old you brush off as "a kid" at work tries to teach you something at the office, don't dismiss him. Remember, he grew up with an iPhone in his hand while you still are searching Google and asking it questions as though it's Ask Jeeves.

The second thing to mention is why I felt bad after running into Steve. This was because, when he asked my mother and me that morning if we'd seen anything interesting, I rattled off some warblers and, "I think a Red-eyed Vireo." Sorry, Steve. My lack of knowledge got me again. This time not out of an inflated sense of experience in identification but, rather, my inexperience.

The sighting reinforced, just like another bird had about two weeks before, that anything is possible. And trust me when I say, anything. Because you're talking to a guy (or reading the words of a guy) who not even a month ago, was out of work, had just written a poignant and emotional blog about accepting that the Marriott chapter of my career was over when, out of nowhere, I received an email from a former colleague, one I'd never worked with directly, asking me if I was still looking for work. I have since told Blair, my now-boss but then just a "person I emailed from time to time," that I replied with "yes," before I even read the entire email. I'm only slightly exaggerating.

I want to save some of the "fine-print" details of my return to work, and the circumstances by which it happened, for the final chapter but I'd be remiss if I didn't take this opportunity to say, while I am still not an expert on birding, which I admitted to in the opening sentences of this book, I do know a thing or two about possibilities. And believing in them. The Black-billed Cuckoo that turned out not to be a Red-eyed Vireo is proof. So is another bird in the Vireo family, the Black-whiskered.

About two weeks before the Cuckoo sighting, I found myself at the Botanical Garden on a Thursday afternoon, after I had started working. I had dropped the boys off at the Plantation Preserve for a golf lesson but for whatever reason, I didn't feel up for the walk that day. Remember, this is where I said the Botanical Garden provided for a nice alternative when time was a factor. It was also a nice alternative when energy was a factor as well. I had been back at work for about two weeks and was mentally drained as I readjusted to the grind that I mentioned in the chapter on perspective. My bosses were gracious with giving me ample ramp-up time but at the end of the day, when you go back to work, it's time to get to work.

I strolled around the Botanical Garden, again in a leisurely way just appreciating anything and everything I was seeing. A Blue-Jay trying his best to crack open a peanut. A Tricolored Heron and a  White Ibis sitting in a tree together like old friends. And then, something else that looked not so familiar. I took a few photos of this unknown bird, then a few more of some others before heading out to pick up the boys.

When I got home later that evening, you know the drill. Though this time, I did for one reason or another, upload the photo of the unfamiliar species to one of my trusty apps. It suggested a Black-whiskered Vireo. At this point, I knew of only a few Vireo species common in this part of Florida at this time of year. The aforementioned Red-eyed that turns out I didn't know well enough, as well as the White-eyed Vireo and the Yellow-throated Vireo. When it comes to rare species, even eBird doesn't list them as an option when submitting sightings. You have to enter it and they need to confirm it based on the photos, until you get "credit." I suppose, yet again, it does make sense to prove rare as opposed to assume rare. So, again, my point is that when sites such as eBird don't even list something that one is likely to find in the area, this type of bird—such as a

Black-billed Cuckoo, Bahama Mockingbird or Black-whiskered Vireo—is not even on my radar. In my still. somewhat-of-a-beginner state, I don't know enough about non-Florida birds to look for some of them.

After the app suggestion and having learned from the past, I then uploaded the photo to the Florida-based group where the reaction was similar to what it would be two weeks later with the Cuckoo  sighting. Unlike with that one, I posted it with the question: "Is this a Black-whiskered Vireo," perhaps in an attempt to seem like I knew what the heck I was talking about. In any case, it was confirmed and, once again, pointed out by many to be rare. Common in the Caribbean, they can be found here on the rarest of occasions in the southernmost parts of Florida. Broward then might be as far "north" as you'll ever see one.

As you can see, it indeed does have what appears to be a black mustache—a Fu Manchu that would make even Hulk Hogan jealous. Yet another reminder, on possibilities.

One final tidbit I will share as it relates to possibilities is, oftentimes, these possibilities that we happen upon have been there all along, almost hiding in plain sight, as the expression goes. One day maybe a month into our weekly walks at Plantation Preserve in June, my mom suggested an alternative: Plantation Central Park. Unlike the Preserve (which I had been close to while playing golf), as well as the other parks I have shared that I never knew were there, Central Park on the other hand, is a place I have probably spent more time than any other since moving to Florida.

It's where my sons play baseball, flag football and tennis, and where all three of my kids have attended summer camp the past five years. While I had been to Central Park countless times since 2013, never without rushing to the ball field, or running from Dylan's practice or game to Noah's, or darting out of the park in time to get Emma from gymnastics. Certainly, never to enjoy a leisurely stroll to embrace nature and conversation with my mother.

But that day, I saw dozens of birds, presumably all of which had been there for years, and once again, I never took the time to notice. To appreciate. To listen. The highlight was seeing a Burrowing Owl, but not where one would normally expect to find one—a hole in the ground, as its name suggests. The Florida Fish & Wildlife Commission has designated nesting locations set up throughout Broward County that are "roped off" by white piping and signs to caution those to avoid disrupting their slumber. But if you walk by when they're out of the burrow, you can view them fairly easily and, yes, Central Park is one of those locations that has several of the nesting spots.

I didn't see one that day when looking for one in his burrow. Before I could even be disappointed, I looked up and not even five feet from Baseball Field 5, where both my sons have played dozens  of games, there he was, perched on a tree. He was sitting there as if that "wise old owl" was waiting for me, like many of the others that followed that summer would be, to offer his words of wisdom and encouragement. And since Baseball Field 5 was silent that day, and there were no practices to rush to, I finally took the time to listen to what he was saying. And, since it was toward the early end of my weekly walks with my mom, I would do the same with all the other little (and big) birds that offered their own words of wisdom over the next several months.

Today, while I am grateful to be back at work, blessed to have a supportive family, and thankful for everything I have, and the lessons learned these last few months that I will continue to learn and remember for the rest of my life—as I have shared many times before and will continue to do—I am aware that so many others are not as fortunate. This, by the way, is always the mindset to have. Just like I said that it shouldn't take a pandemic for employers to show more empathy, well, it shouldn't take one for any of us to realize that we should be more grateful for what we have as opposed to complaining about what we don't.

I share all of that to say, during some of my more challenging moments during the dog days of summer, when my mind started to wander to sometimes dark and sad places, I'd try my best to quickly snap out of it and remember the lesson on possibilities.

For anyone reading this who, like I was not so long ago, is looking for answers, looking for something, looking for possibilities no matter the situation, 10 years from now when COVID-19 is hopefully a far distant memory—but anytime you find yourself clinging to hope, wondering when your next chapter will start or when that next door will open, just remember, a Bald Eagle may be sitting right around the corner.

Or, better yet, a Black-whiskered Vireo. The possibility always exists, even if it seems as though it doesn't. It always exists. It always will. Sometimes we just need to stop and pay attention and see the Burrowing Owl away from his burrow, perched on a tree, eager to pass on his wisdom to us. And sometimes we simply need to close our eyes and take a breath before we unknowingly stumble upon that Black-billed Cuckoo, just waiting to be discovered.

Chapter 13

PEACE AND APPRECIATION FOR THE JOURNEY: THE BLUE JAY

*"You've taken hundreds of pictures of Blue Jays,
why are you stopping to take one now?"*
— My Son, Dylan

The Blue Jay taken August 21, 2020, at Cypress Hammock Park, Coral Springs, Florida.

I feel the need to clarify before I go further that the image chosen for the title page of this chapter, much like the Summer Tanager, was not chosen for the quality of the photograph. In fact, the opposite. And it serves as a great illustration for the lesson I am about to share.

On August 21, Noah was getting ready for his turn for a sleepover with Grammy (my mom) like Emma would be a couple weeks later when she missed out on our unsuccessful mission to find the Red-headed Woodpecker. This time, Emma was excited about a girl's afternoon with mom and so Dylan and I were about to do what we don't do often enough. What I don't do often enough with any of my three children for that matter— have some one-on-one time. Yes, this would include visiting a park for birding but, unlike some of our mission-specific trips, this was one of those occasions, where it was genuinely about the time we'd be spending together—the 20 minutes in the car each way, and the hour or so we'd have to walk and talk.

Dylan, like many who have younger siblings (or older ones in some cases), can be a totally different person when he is in a one-on-one situation. There would be no sibling rivalry, no need to feel the need to fight for attention, and no need to put on a front for anyone. This is why I appreciate these moments as much as I do, and what makes me realize I need more of them. Why he needs more of them, too, because "Dylan, great job for getting an A on your math test," doesn't immediately need to include a follow-up of, "Emma, terrific job participating and showing confidence today," and, "Noah, I am proud of you for staying focused and getting all your work done today."

As parents, we feel the need, and rightly so, to ensure that none of our kids feel neglected, or not appreciated or unrecognized but sometimes we, or at least I, overdo it. Going back to a previous lesson and my "love language" indicating I am a "Words of Affirmation" person, perhaps I try to compensate when I feel one is getting more of the spotlight at any given time than my other two children. Sometimes, though, they *do* need to stand alone, to be treated as an individual and made to feel special as a person first, not part of a trio.

I don't remind myself of this importance often enough and so it is during those infrequent occasions when I realize just how much it means to him to have my attention without it quickly being taken away by someone else. Again, another carryover lesson on being present. It means a lot to me, too, by the way.

On the drive that day, in typical Dylan fashion, he asked me thoughtful questions about anything and everything, and this would continue after we arrived. Dylan has always been notorious, going back to his earliest days of preschool, for asking me questions that I have always described as the kind that keep me awake at night. I think, "How does his brain work like that," and, no, not complex math equations or science questions—he asks plenty of those too, and as I usually tell him, "You're asking the wrong guy."

No, I am talking about poignant, philosophical, wise-beyond-his-years types of questions. So, this was another one of those days where our conversations were filled with those sorts of, "Gee, Dylan. Great question," type discussions and he's always (or usually) very patient with me as I wax poetic for far longer than necessary.

As we roamed around Cypress Hammock Park that day in Coral Springs, the conversation shifted from one topic to another, when all the sudden we came upon a tree with, not a rare or unexpected species, but an expected one. A guaranteed one almost. A Blue Jay. The same Blue Jay that is featured on the title page of this chapter in a photo that I admitted wasn't my best. It's, in fact, probably one of my worst photographs of a Blue Jay. I mean, you can't even see his face. You've already seen one of my better ones. I shared it last chapter when I described it as him trying his best to crack open a peanut as he pecked at it over and over as if he were doing his best impression of a Woodpecker.

So, this photo was not chosen because it is considered the centerpiece of my Blue Jay photo album. It was chosen because it not only represents the lesson that I am going to spend the rest of this chapter discussing but also because it represents the answer to one of Dylan's other questions that day, one he likely asked, not realizing it was as philosophical as I chose to interpret it. After I delightfully pointed out that Blue Jay perched on a tree right in front of where we were standing, Dylan said, "Dad, we see 10 Blue Jays a day in our backyard. You've taken hundreds of pictures of Blue Jays. Why are you stopping to take one now?"

I could have answered with, "Because, I feel like it." It would've satisfied many kids, but not Dylan. Either way, it would not have satisfied me, especially because I had a better answer, and it ties back to some of what I started to articulate in previous chapters—remember the "Oh, it's just an Anhinga" mindset I had at one point? By this time, though, I was a couple more months into it, had experienced some new challenges, and had the benefit of the learnings that I've shared in all the pages of this book thus far—all of this led me to interpret and answer the question the way I chose.

First, one additional tidbit about that afternoon. I mentioned very early on in the book, how a few of the jobs that I interviewed for seemed to stack up into a pile of rejections. I have only shared the details of one thus far and it was the phone call I received the day the boys and I saw the two Crested Caracaras. That was, by far, the most challenging of the job-rejection experiences. This one I am about to share didn't feel as agonizing simply because I hadn't invested nearly as much time in it. Nevertheless, another blow that came at an inopportune time but as I share this story, perhaps more opportune than I realized then.

While we were in Hilton Head at the beginning part of August, I continued to apply for jobs online. One of them was based in Boca Raton in Palm Beach County, about 30 minutes north. By then, of course, I was familiar with Palm Beach County based on my numerous birding outings over the past few months. Boca, though, I had been familiar with for years, and we'd been there a lot. If you've ever eaten at a Shake Shack, the middle-upscale burger joint that is the creation of famed restaurateur, Danny Meyer, you'll know what I am talking about. There is one near the Boca Town Square shopping mall, both of which we'd enjoy visiting over the years.

When I saw the posting that day on vacation, I was intrigued when I saw it, and, of course, encouraged when, after we had returned home, I received an email to set up an interview.

Here is the quick synopsis:

Monday, August 17: Interview with the head of recruiting, followed by immediate affirmation the call went well, stating she wanted me to interview with the hiring manager as soon as possible.

Tuesday, August 18: Email from the recruiter setting up an interview for the next day.

Wednesday, August 19: Interview with the hiring manager. I felt great about it. I felt we had established a quick rapport. We had very similar backgrounds; she started out as a journalist, wrote for newspapers, then jumped into the world of corporate communications. The similarity of our career paths was striking.

Thursday, August 20: I sent a follow-up note to the hiring manager, thanking her for her time, and letting her know how much I enjoyed the conversation and appreciated the opportunity to interview for the role. Later that same day, she emailed me back—which is unusual. Oftentimes hiring managers won't do this, perhaps because of what it did to me— gave me a false sense of hope. But I felt I had reason to be hopeful, not only based on my perceptions of our discussion but because she closed her email by saying I should expect to hear back from the recruiter "very soon." Well, she was right about one thing—the very soon part.

Friday, August 21: I was headed out the door. Dylan had his shoes on, and my mom was on her way over to get Noah by 3:30. I wanted to leave before she arrived because, like I said earlier in this chapter, sometimes the sibling rivalry is high, especially when it comes to something like that. I wanted Noah to be able to have his "send-off" without any background noise. I was sitting at my computer and had the inclination to check my email one last time before I left, and there it was—the "very soon" had arrived. 3:09 p.m. "Unfortunately, I'm following up to let you know that the hiring manager has decided to move forward with other candidates. Although we were impressed with your skills/experience ..." followed by a series of words I couldn't even process at the time in my blurred state of mind.

F***, I quietly whispered under my breath before shutting my computer and belting out an exuberant, "Okay, Dylan—let's go!"

This time, unlike the previous rejection, I was more frustrated and in fact almost annoyed more than anything else. I couldn't quite articulate why, especially given that I hadn't invested any time really, but I felt slighted, I guess, is the only way to put it. As in—*other candidates? Impressed with my skills but...*but what? I realize this, too, was likely a form letter response but it came from an actual person. The same person I spoke to four days earlier who excitedly passed me on to the hiring manager for the next interview.

The annoyance dissipated to a flippant "whatever," which then transitioned just as quickly to the sinking feeling that I had felt just weeks before. The same familiar sting of yet another rejection and again, in the midst of an outing with at least one of my kids. In this case, seconds before I was about to leave. After I shut my computer, I told Dylan I was ready, and we were on our way.

The rest of what I wrote above about the drive there and the great conversation was all true. I was able to put it aside and enjoy my time with Dylan. Unlike the incident I keep referring to that took place weeks earlier, this time I was able to compartmentalize it, put it into perspective, and realize that what mattered the most in that moment was spending an afternoon, one on one, with my first-born child for the first time since baseball ended last spring. Nothing else mattered as much.

Now, back to the question.

"Dylan, I'll tell you why. Because, if I can't see a beautiful Blue Jay with its bright and vibrant blue and black and white plumage without feeling the need to at least stop to appreciate it and try to take a photograph to capture the beauty of that moment, then I am missing the point. So, the day that happens—where I no longer feel the need to do that—is the day I know I am not doing this for the right reasons."

He sat quietly for a minute and tried to process my answer before asking, "What do you mean?"

I said, "Think about it this way. I know you like playing Fortnite, but sometimes I'm not so sure based on the way I hear you moaning and groaning from the other room. I know you love to win and trying to win is why we play anything but if you only enjoy playing, *if* you end up winning, then you are going to spend a lot of time miserable while you play it. You have to find joy in playing the game itself, and appreciate playing it, or you're going to be disappointed a lot, because you're not going to win every time."

This lesson I was sharing with Dylan that day was of course based on my own lessons learned and bumps along the way, such as that one night I mentioned in chapter 5 where I realized that it couldn't only be about the number of birds or new species that I'd be able to observe. If it was, I was not only setting myself up for tons of future disappointment, but I was also missing the point. No, it had to be more. It had to be about the adventure itself, the journey itself, not only the destination. Of course, much of what inspired that answer was the email I received right before we left, and the realization that life, much like birding, couldn't only be about the moments of triumph.

This is why I wanted to intercede with the details and added context about the afternoon's events before we left the house, before I told you my answer to Dylan's question. Because, even if I was able to compartmentalize my emotions for him, it didn't mean I hadn't been processing it the entire time on our drive in an attempt to reconcile the millions of emotions swirling in my head. Once I did enter the park with Dylan that day, just like so many other parks on so many other days before it, I felt a sense of peace.

Also, a sense of appreciation for the parks, the places that had become my sanctuaries and seemingly private retreats that provided respites from moments like the one I had just 30 minutes earlier as Dylan and I were about to leave the house. And, for the birds. All of them. Including, yes, the Blue Jay.

Dylan seemed to be getting it, but we continued the conversation as we walked around the park. I mentioned in chapter 4 Dylan's passion for sports, and, again, his passion for winning but I said to him, as much as you love to win—and everyone does—you can't enjoy the sport that you're playing *only* if you win. You must also find pleasure in playing the game itself, and in the journey—even the not so fun parts. You must find a way to appreciate the journey and the battles you fight in your attempt to get that win.

When you find yourself like Drew, in that high school football game in the fall of 2006, in the trenches, grinding for every inch, if you cannot appreciate the struggle and the challenge, how can you truly ever appreciate the accomplishment and the triumph?

The Major League regular season, for example, is 162 games. One hundred. Sixty. Two. That means, on average, these guys are playing just about every other day—if you look at the season as lasting the full year, but it doesn't. They play 162 games over the course of less than six months. In the midst of summer. It's grueling. And, if you're on a team that, by the All-Star Break in July, is already pretty much out of the playoff race? Yeah, those guys better be in it for more than the World Series ring.

And they are. They are in it for the chance to win one game—the next one and then the one that takes place tomorrow, even though they know neither would lead to the World Series, at least not that year but it might lead to one next year. Because they're learning. They're growing. They're getting better. They're embracing the challenges—with their teammates—that will help make them a better ball player so that when the day comes, and a World Series is on the line, they'll be more prepared for it and even more grateful and appreciative because of the days spent grinding, not sure there would ever be this type of pay off one day.

As I type this chapter, my older brother, John, who I mentioned is in his first season as an assistant football coach at Florida State University, earned his first win as part of the Seminoles staff. He took the role knowing it was a "rebuilding" process, a journey, and a long one. When I mentioned in another chapter that he was part of a National Championship winning team in 2007, there were obviously also moments in his career where he and his colleagues knew that the opportunity to achieve that kind of success would not be possible. Again, at least not that year. But you work hard, take some lumps, learn from the lessons, and try to get better every day, knowing it's a part of the overall journey and understanding the perseverance, patience, and humility needed to achieve that level again.

You don't need to be a coach or a player to understand this. In fact, if you really want to understand the importance of appreciation of the journey, ask a fan—especially fans of teams who never win a title, at least not in their lifetime. Yet, it doesn't stop them from enjoying their team or dampen their passion for the team, the game, the possibilities—yes, the possibilities—and the journey itself.

My grandfather on my mother's side, her father, Lawrence Penn, was one of my biggest role models in life and his name is Dylan's middle name. He died about a month before I graduated from college in 2003. A lifelong, die-hard Boston Red Sox fan born in 1934, he also died about 18 months before the Sox won their first World Series title since 1918, following an 86-year drought that is often attributed to the Curse of the Bambino, suggesting that the Red Sox were being punished for trading away one of the game's all-time greatest players, Babe Ruth, to the New York Yankees.

Eighty-six years? Talk about appreciating and embracing the journey from a fan perspective. Because, again, hundreds if not thousands of players would wear the Boston uniform over those years, some for a season or two, but for the fans like my Grandpa—they didn't have a choice. They were in it for the long haul no matter what. By the way, the Blue Jay, incidentally, is the mascot of a team in the Red Sox division, for those that didn't know—the Toronto Blue Jays.

After Boston traded Ruth away, the Yankees would go on to win dozens of titles over the years while the Sox seemed to get close to tasting success from time to time, only to have it taken away in the blink of an eye. If a Major League Baseball season is a marathon, for a 69-year-old Red Sox fan who had never seen their team win a title, that must feel like, well, 69 marathons, I guess. Anyway, the fact that they won it all one year after he died seemed cruel, but I have the front page of the Boston Globe from October 26, 2004, framed in my home office. The headline from that paper's game story said it all: YES!

YES, indeed, and this is a great example on appreciation and finding peace and joy in the journey not the destination. Because you're likely not going to find a more passionate fanbase in all of sports than that of the Boston Red Sox, and for people like my grandfather, who never got to see them win it all, it couldn't only be about the end result. He spent 69 years just loving the Red Sox, not because they won, but because he loved them and believed that someday they could win again. Remember, the possibilities always exist.

When we find ourselves, much like I did earlier that summer, somewhat stale, it's in those moments when we must stop and pause and remember to embrace the process. Embrace the challenges and the struggles along the way, too. The mistakes, the lessons, the hiccups after we've learned them. Each lead to growth and progress and get us one step closer to the destination. And even though we will never reach it, we never stop trying to.

Certainly, we aren't going to find joy *all* the time. We aren't going enjoy every moment. There will be disappointment along the way, but we need to look at those disappointments within the broader context and appreciate all of it as part of the journey. We must appreciate the journey we are on while we are on it, not only in hindsight when we find ourselves sitting around one day and think, "Why didn't I take the time to stop and take that photo of a Blue Jay when I had the chance?" That is why I was standing there that day taking photos of one, and why I chose the only half decent one I took that day for the title page of this chapter.

As Dylan and I wandered around some more, we saw a few fall migrants, but truth be told, I don't really remember most of the others. Again, that day, it was about the appreciation for the journey, the appreciation for some special one-one-one time with Dylan, and, like I said, not much else mattered. Until we got in the car.

While I did a good job compartmentalizing my emotions

from the email that I had received the seconds before we left the house, and the conversation continued during the drive home, my mind, like it had throughout the summer, began to wander. Almost like the 10-year-old me or however old I was, not wanting to return to school after winter break. It's as if I knew as soon as I pulled into my driveway, the reality of having to have another "not meant to be" and "well, back to the drawing board" conversation with myself would hit me.

As I said, this sting was a little less potent, but potent, nonetheless. Because at that point, a job, any job, would have been welcomed but this one seemed to have so many positive signs. Signs that seemed to point in the right direction but, for whatever reason, I was going the wrong way down the street. Remember when I said the universe doesn't ever conspire against us? I said it in the chapter on positivity, and I believe this. I believe it now, and I believed it then, but it does not mean we are immune to feeling pain.

While I didn't think anything larger was at play, in terms of a cosmic jinx, I was still starting to wonder, what did I do wrong? And I mean that about the actual interviews I had been on—all of them. Did I talk too much? Did I not look directly into the camera during the video interview? Did I not give concrete enough examples? Like, please, just help a guy out, I am grasping at straws here. And those "thanks, but no thanks" emails don't seem to give us any closure at all. And so, because they don't, they make us have those, "why me? What did I do?" thoughts.

I wish we could respond to them and say, "Please, just let me know. In the interest of pursuing excellence, give me something that I can take and learn from, so next time I am fortunate enough to have an interview, I can put my best foot forward."

On that drive home, I wanted to tell Dylan about it all. I almost started to. The reason I didn't is not because I didn't think he could handle it. At 10 years old I knew he could. In fact, all my kids had been supportive all summer. One day back in April maybe, I had one of my first interviews during the stretch, one I haven't mentioned yet, and the only reason I am now is for the following anecdote. After the interview finished, as I would sometimes do, I went outside and sat on the back patio and took a few minutes to collect my thoughts and regroup, which usually means, relive the play by play from the conversation in my head. Anyway, Emma came outside after me, and said, "Dad, guess what?" And, before I could even say what, she said, "But first, how was your job call?" Wow. The wherewithal it takes to know how to do that sort of thing at then-five years old. Pretty remarkable.

So, yes, I knew Dylan would be fine with handling the

news and hearing me talk about it. I just didn't want Kristie to somehow hear it from him and not me. We pulled into the driveway, and as predicted, my mindset started to shift downward as soon as I saw my laptop sitting on the dining room table.

I kept it to myself for just about the rest of the evening in a misguided attempt to be selfless, and not ruin everyone's Friday night. To not let others see my pain and then feel it, too. I knew Kristie was holding down the fort, and while she never once put pressure on me or made me feel bad about anything, again, it didn't stop me from feeling bad enough for myself. So, I kept quiet, and likely would have, until Kristie saw me moping around and called me out on my mood after I was snippy at one point in the evening.

It was Friday night, we were hanging out as a family (minus Noah), so what gives? Like I said earlier, this time the rejection brought about an odd mix of sadness and self-doubt combined with annoyance and frustration that almost teetered into the anger category. Again, not about *this* job. Not about the one before it but about everything. When I mentioned last chapter that sometimes we just have to bow our heads and pray to something, this was about as close as I got to hitting my knees and offering my soul to whoever wanted it.

August 21 was arguably the hardest night of the entire

summer out of work. Somehow, in that one email received at 3:09 p.m., it symbolized the series of rejections, desperation for answers, and the continued inner-struggle I faced almost all summer. I found myself feeling guilty for having all those feelings when I knew so many others still had it worse.

Still, even though we are cognitively aware that others have it worse, it doesn't always make us feel better, and what I've come to learn is that it's okay. Each of us is allowed to hurt and feel bad in our own relative way. There is no hierarchy of sadness. We are all allowed to feel. In fact, I came across an article while researching some of this that same weekend. I went back and found the article, "Why it's OK to grieve small losses during the coronavirus pandemic," written by Samantha Turnbull.

The article opened with the following statement that immediately resonated with me. "My heavy heart and guilty head are in a strange tug of war." Yes. Exactly this.

The term "cancel culture" seems to be the biggest buzzword of this political season and overall social environment. I am not even sure I know what it means. So, the only reason I mentioned it is because I think I am ready to introduce a new one. Our society's biggest culture problem is another C word, in fact. We have a "comparison culture." We always have. In some ways, this is unavoidable.

We take five movies and pit them against each other and

then pick one as the best every year at the Oscars but, how can you compare *Forrest Gump* and *Pulp Fiction?* (Both 1995 Oscar nominees for Best Picture). You can't, really, yet we do, and we celebrate the winner every February. We do this with everyday life situations, too, and in most cases the comparisons are not apples to apples. At least the Academy Awards are choosing only movies. Sometimes, in life, we do things that feel like we are pitting a movie against a music album.

Imagine this fictional conversation for a moment.

"Oh, man. I am so sad that my favorite TV show just got canceled."

"Oh, really? My two-week cruise vacation just got canceled, so who cares about your little television show?"

"Wow, you both sound petty. I lost my job and am worried about putting food on the table. But sorry about your problems."

Here's the thing. Yes, Person A and B probably should be a little more self-aware about vocalizing some of their sadness in front of Person C, and we can hope this wouldn't happen in real life. I chose to make it an actual conversation for this chapter for illustrative purposes. While, yes, I would agree that we should exercise discretion and tact when complaining in front of others, it doesn't mean we aren't allowed to ever express sadness or pain over our own problems, no matter how big or little they appear to be by comparison. Because there is no need to compare.

"People think there's a hierarchy to suffering, and if the thing that's causing you disappointment is lower on the hierarchy, we have this tendency to dismiss our emotions," said Psychologist Lea Waters, from the Centre for Positive Psychology at the University of Melbourne, who was quoted in the article, while also stating we need to give ourselves permission to be disappointed. She also said, just like what had happened to me that Friday night, when we do keep it in and repress it—out of guilt or in an attempt to protect and shield others—we then end up having it pour out in a more explosive way than it would have if we just let our guard down and gave ourselves permission to feel.

After reading that, I felt a little better about my feelings of sadness and grief and knew that I didn't have to feel as guilty. I spent a lot of time that weekend lost in so many different thoughts, and kicking different scenarios in my head—should we consider moving again? Who moves during a pandemic? Who *hires* during a pandemic? Ultimately, my mind always went back to that same place—work—and finding it soon. On that weekend, back to that specific job opportunity and a specific place, too. Boca. I mentioned it was a place we had visited frequently since moving to Florida but not for the burgers or birds.

When my dad's father was still alive, my Papou that I

referenced earlier, he had a condo in Boca where he'd live half the year and had done so since I was about 20 years old. Yes, like many his age, he was a snowbird. He died in 2015 but I am thankful for the two years we lived in Florida while he was still living, because it gave my boys the chance to spend more time with their great-grandfather that they likely wouldn't have had otherwise, and it allowed my daughter the opportunity to spend her first Thanksgiving, in 2014, with him when he was at our house for dinner when she was about five months old.

In any case, the thought of Boca, in general, made me think about both him and my other grandfather, yes, the lifelong Red Sox fan who never got to experience the glory of a World Series.

I thought about them both, not only that weekend, but throughout the last few months. Because while I was, of course, blessed—as I have mentioned so many times before—to have a supportive family in my corner all the time, sometimes a grandfather can be a boy's, or man's, most influential advisor. People of their generation, often referred to as the Greatest Generation, and for good reason, were cut from a different cloth. My Papou, Charles, fought in WWII and earned both a Purple Heart and Bronze Star for his years of service, yet like all who fought in that war, never spoke about it, let alone brag.

My Grandpa, Larry, served in the Air Force, never went to college, yet scraped and clawed his way to eventually become a district leader for the beverage company he spent his life dedicated to. He was 6 foot 2 inches, but it wasn't his physical presence alone that made him seem so strong. He was the kind of guy who walked into a room and you knew he was there. He was the epitome of strength.

When I found myself out of work for those few months, I thought how great it would be to pick up the phone and call either one. Don't get me wrong, I wasn't looking for an "everything's going to be okay," type of call with either. I had that. I had been hearing that for months, and, yes, it did reassure me and make me feel better but, sometimes, you also need a jolt in the arm that men of that era could provide because they didn't pull punches.

In fact, when I was fooling around in my early teen years, my Papou once said to me, during a family gathering, "You're going to be the first Papuchis not to graduate college." I tell this story to my own kids once in a while. They always have the same reaction, "That was mean." I tell them I had that same reaction, too, at the time but he didn't say it to be mean, this I know. Because as much as we need the "everything will be okay" messages, sometimes we need to hear the "stop moping around and, pick your head up, roll up your sleeves, embrace the struggle, embrace the challenges, and get up to fight another day" messages, too.

Yes, embrace the journey. Before I close this chapter and move to my final lesson, I want to share a few thoughts on the concept of embracing the journey. There is a reason why I chose to include some additional details about these two role models in my life.

It's because when I talk about the concept of finding peace and joy and appreciation for the journey itself, I've come to realize that my journey did not start seven months ago when I found myself out of work. It didn't start five months ago when I developed a passion for birding. It started 40 years ago. The summer trips to Ocean City. The little league championships. The last-minute book reports. (Wait, there was more than one? Sadly, the answer is probably yes). The laughs, the tears, the wins, and the losses, and the incredible people who were with me every step of the way. And those who still are. The people who have shaped my life and still shape it every day—from my 89-year-old grandmother to my six-year-old daughter.

Because it is the sum of my entire life's journey thus far, not just the last few months, that enabled me to find peace, find perspective, find patience, and perseverance. It's not just the last few months that taught me to embrace the possibilities the lay before me if I keep an open mind and a positive outlook.

It was everyone with me—both physically and spiritually. Including a Red Sox fan, who was with me when I learned to love and appreciate a Blue Jay.

Chapter 14

PAYING IT FORWARD AND FINDING BALANCE AS THE JOURNEY CONTINUES: THE BLACK-THROATED BLUE WARBLER

"Finally sharing what the little birdie told me. All of them"— Me

The Black-throated Blue Warbler taken October 4, 2020, at Fern Forest Nature Preserve, Coconut Creek, Florida.

It was Wednesday, August 26, 2020. Five days prior, I received the rejection email from the company I had interviewed with earlier that week. I just posted on LinkedIn, following that email, I was open to work. I had done that from time to time during those few months, in addition to the blogs I was writing and the jobs I was posting for, as a way to continue to stoke the fire, if you will. I started doing this back in April, in fact, and the first time I did it, I felt quite vulnerable. Sort of like, "Hey guys, just wanted to let you know I still haven't found a job yet."

Of course, that wasn't the tone of the message, but I suppose finding myself that honest about my story, that early on, was what allowed me to keep writing and with that same level of realness and vulnerability that seemed to resonate so well with so many. I wasn't ashamed and didn't feel shame or view it as a stigma. I wanted others who may have also been reluctant to do the same, feel reassurance it was okay to do, even if it seemed uncomfortable.

In addition to the "looking for work" reminder, I had just written what I considered my farewell to Marriott blog on LinkedIn—one of the most positively received articles I'd written. It made me feel good but there is some irony in reading messages like, "You've given me hope," when I found that I was, at times, still looking for it myself. Still looking for...possibilities.

Little did I know, it would appear out of nowhere, just like the Cooper's Hawk darting by me at the Plantation Preserve as I was already done for the day and headed to my car. I was sitting at my dining room table when I got an email from a familiar name, Blair, as I mentioned last chapter. I immediately recognized her name and then my eyes zeroed in on the subject line: Potential Opportunity. Given the events of the last few months, the past few weeks in particular, I opened it, cautiously optimistic. I don't know who coined that term, by the way, but I am thankful it was created, because it truly was the perfect way to describe my feelings at that moment. I wanted to be hopeful, but I had one eyebrow raised at the same time.

As I said in the last chapter, I responded to her before I finished reading. She wrote me back right away and we set up a call for the next day. By the time the call ended, one that I envisioned to be exploratory, on Thursday, August 27, she essentially verbally offered me the job. I was stunned as I hung up the phone. Her final words were along the lines of, "How soon can you start?"

If I thought my mind had been racing the previous weekend, wow. Less than one week after the hardest night during the time I was out of work. Never in a million years did I think it would happen, and certainly not like that. A woman I never worked with but crossed paths with off and on, emailed me out of nowhere, and by the time we hung up the phone, I was making plans to rejoin Marriott. Unbelievable. There is no other word.

I walked back into the house (this time I'd taken the call outside), looked at Kristie, and said, "Well, it looks like I might be going back to Marriott." Never stop believing in the possibilities.

I'll pause here since I just mentioned her. Kristie was as supportive a spouse during these few months as any I could imagine. She never pressured me about finding work, though I know it was weighing on her mind. She has always been more mindful of finances than me, and I know that sort of thing stresses her out. Yet, she never let it show to me because she probably knew it would put more pressure on me to find work than I was already putting on myself. In fact, if you remember something I wrote in the preface—I felt like I wasn't providing for my family but learned to accept that I was providing in a new, but still important, way by being more present for my children. This was her commentary, and when she saw me getting hard on myself, she helped to remind me of this from time to time. Still, when the news came in, I knew she was as relieved as I was, and just as excited for me, too.

Because of some internal processes that needed to take place, plus the Labor Day holiday the following week, I ended up starting September 14, when it was all said and done.

After I finalized everything, I sent my new boss a text. "Blair, I don't know what I did to make you reach out to me when you did, but please know, I'll be eternally grateful, and I'll work my butt off for you!"

She responded by saying she had heard good things about my work but one thing in particular stood out the most, "You also have a great reputation for being a nice guy."

Let me tell you this much. If you remember only one sentence out of this entire book, please let it be that one. Above all else, it starts by being nice.

It was Thursday, September 4, when I signed the paperwork and I'd start my new job 10 days later. My boys were taking their first in a series of golf lessons my mom and Rick graciously signed them up for at Plantation Preserve, once we learned fall sports were not going to happen. We knew that after several months without it, they needed some sort of organized physical activity in their lives, especially since Emma had gymnastics.

Remember when I said I was fortunate to have the support network I had? Yes, this is true. Knowing I wouldn't have been in the financial position to do so at the time, they offered to sign them up before I found work. I appreciate the generosity of those so close to me, and I promise to pay it forward. Which is what this chapter is about.

I dropped the boys at 4:00 p.m. that Thursday, and I

headed to an old familiar place. In truth, it's a relatively new, yet still familiar place, but it felt like home. As I entered the trail I realized, for the first time in what felt like forever, I had 90 minutes alone at the Preserve. In hindsight, that may have been *the* most time I ever had there alone.

As I walked along the trail that day, my mind began to wander. My eBird list would be fairly modest that afternoon because this walk, like many others had been, was more about the journey than the destination. My mind then raced at points as I tried to wrap my head around the events that transpired in the last week or so that resulted in me returning to work.

My mind then began to wander even more, and I almost got teary-eyed (again, not afraid to show emotion) but they weren't for the same reasons as the ones before. The tears that day were that of gratitude and relief, with a million other emotions swirling around my head—joy, appreciation, humility, and disbelief, among them.

Then, I started to think of the birds. It was that day, in that moment, somewhere around trail marker 300, that I had the revelation—It was the birds. It was the birds who saved my spirit, my soul, my sanity, and maybe even saved my life, in many respects. I know this sounds dramatic but it's true. And when, what felt like the weight of the world, had finally lifted off my shoulders that Thursday afternoon, it hit me for the first time, just how much I owed to them these last several months. My "friends" who taught and reinforced lessons that will make me a more understanding, and hopefully better, employee, parent, spouse, partner, friend, and person.

And, if you remember the final words I wrote in the preface, I said I wanted to share my story and these lessons because it might make you a little more understanding, and, perhaps, a little "better" at those things, too. And, so, since I cannot pay back the birds what I owe them for the help, hope, and belief in the possibilities they provided me these last several months, this is how I am paying it forward. On their behalf.

So, it was on this first Thursday in September, one month ago today as I write this chapter, that the thought to write this book popped into my head. While I was well aware of some of the lessons I was learning, some of which I posted on LinkedIn, it wasn't until I was walking along the trail that day alone, I started to add it all up. From the Limpkin to the Prairie Warbler, I realized right then and there what a profound impact this activity-turned-passion had on me during this time. In addition to the therapeutic nature of the hobby itself, the number of learnings it provided me these past few months would be too incredible of a story not to share. So, it was settled, I'd get home that night and write about it, and finally share "what the little birdie told me"—all of them.

This book was going to be another blog post until I quickly realized this story deserved more. The birds deserved more. And I wanted the people who are still looking for their next door to open, those still wondering if it's okay to believe in possibilities, to have this book. For today and whenever they start to wonder those things. I want to have it, too. I'll put it next to the picture of the Northern Cardinal that my mom framed for me for my fortieth birthday with the words "Find Your Cardinal" across the top.

Now that I've found mine, I wanted others to find theirs, too. And, for you to find yours as well. The day I sat down to write this final chapter was Sunday, October 4, 2020. I thought to myself, "Tomorrow is the start of week four back at work. Wow." It's been a full spectrum of emotions, but I can share with you the one lesson I had to learn after I went back to work, and, thus, the last lesson I will share with you on these pages: balance.

As I mentioned in the story about finding the Black-billed Cuckoo, my birding adventures have gone from four or five times a week to once or twice. Emma is now back at gymnastics five days a week, and the there is talk that the city will be opening for winter baseball in November, and the county school system is readying for the kids to return later this month. While I am beyond thankful to be back at work—which I cannot state often enough—there is still some sadness that comes with the thought of life returning to normal.

The other day, during a routine trip to Publix—still in mesh shorts—I walked down the baking aisle and saw the shelves stocked with flour, sugar, and every other baking supply you could imagine. It made me a little nostalgic and wistful as it brought me back to the earliest days of quarantine, when those same shelves were empty as every would-be baker in South Florida, just like me, was making the most of their quarantine time, too.

It brought me right back to that time and place when I thought it would last just a few weeks, I'd be working within a month, and nothing else was as important as the ability to have those bonus moments with the kids that we will never get back—baking, playing, laughing, and spending time together.

When my kids look back at the summer of 2020, the first thing that likely comes to their mind would be "birds," with maybe just a hint of a grimace but, with any hope, there is a good possibility when you ask them this same question in 20 years, the answer won't change but their facial expression will.

Nevertheless, these last few months we cannot get back—just like I said in the chapter about time. It never gets easier accepting this, and, in fact, it gets harder. But I can say, we not only made the most of these times but learned one of the most valuable lessons of all, yes—balance. We may not be able to stay in our bunkers forever, shielded from the day-to-day responsibilities and commitments that make our lives complete, but we cannot allow ourselves to be weighed down by them either and go back to a world where we don't have a second to breathe. We must not give up on other things that may interest us and ignore other passions and hobbies for the sake of just one. The best example I can give on the lesson of balance is this story.

After Rick signed the boys up for the Golf Academy at Plantation Preserve, he signed himself up for 10 private one-on-one lessons with one of the golf pros, Barry. After four lessons, he realized the one-hour sessions were a little too much for his knee—he's having knee replacement surgery at the end of this month. Rather than ask Barry for a refund, he asked if he could gift his six remaining lessons to family: two to my mom, two to the boys (one each) to go along with their weekly group lesson, and two to me. Once again, I am fortunate.

On Tuesday, September 29, 2020, I showed up at the Plantation Preserve for the first time in six months not for the birds, but for golf. At 40 years old, I had my first golf lesson after years of just hitting balls at the range. Thus, I was still searching for little birdies but of a different variety. And for many, if not most, much rarer and more elusive than the feathered kind!

Barry has an expression, "Every golfer dreams of one day hitting that Nirvana shot." Perhaps this hobby, too, provides the chance for possibilities, for pushing our boundaries, for the continuous pursuit of excellence, and, as I soon found out, patience.

We got to work and, just like on May 21 when I found the Northern Cardinal with my mom, the sounds of metal clubs hitting golf balls could be heard. Only this time, they were mine. And just like that day in May, the sounds of birds chirping filled the air, too. But this time, they were off in the distance. I smiled as I heard them and returned to my stance, found my grip, and hit, not quite a Nirvana shot—because crawl before walk, remember? But, still, a pretty darn good one.

I left that day content. Fulfilled. Happy. I didn't see one bird.

Balance. And a pretty decent 100-yard shot with my pitching wedge.

As I write the final words of this chapter and of this book that encapsulates the last several months (and in some ways encapsulates my 40 years on earth thus far), it is, as stated above, Sunday evening, October 4, one month to the day I signed on the dotted line to return to work.

The photo I chose for the title page of this final chapter, like all the others, was chosen for a reason and what it represents. Like those others, it will serve as a reminder of the journey, such as the Blue Jay that reminded me it's about having an appreciation for the journey itself that matters the most, not necessarily the result.

The Great Egret and the Ovenbird that taught me, on any journey, I must remind myself it's okay to learn to crawl before I start to walk.

The Spot-breasted Oriole that reminded me about the importance of perseverance, and the American Redstart that reminded me to be patient, and that good things come to those who wait.

The Roseate Spoonbill that will always remind me that finding a passion for something will inspire me in new and unexpected ways.

The Yellow-crowned Night Heron that made me realize there are exceptions to every rule, but they are just that and that time is precious and shouldn't be taken for granted.

The Crested Caracara that reinforced with me, when I step out from beyond my own backyard, I open myself to new and exciting opportunities.

The Florida Scrub-Jay that reminded me of the importance of preparation and doing my homework, and the Red-headed Woodpecker that reminded me what happens when I don't—wherever he is out there.

The Blue-gray Gnatcatcher that reinforced the importance of staying present and giving something or someone my full focus and attention.

The Prairie Warbler that is there, and always will be, to remind me to keep pushing, practicing, and pursing excellence.

The Northern Mockingbird that reminded me to not only see a different perspective but be open and willing to sometimes change mine, especially if I want to see an Indigo Bunting.

The Summer Tanager that let me know it's okay to not know everything, and that listening to the guidance and wisdom of others is not a sign of weakness.

The Black-billed Cuckoo that reminded me, when I least expect it, anything can happen because anything is always possible.

And the Northern Cardinal that reminded me that a positive mindset and an optimistic outlook can help me find light during some of my darkest moments.

Plus, the many others, not just those who appeared on the title pages of this book but the more than 100 different species I observed and photographed since May 2020. All of them are there to remind me of the lessons learned, the lessons I will continue to learn, and the lessons I am proud to share with others as I continue my journey and pay it forward.

But the one chosen for this chapter's photo is a little different than the others. Unlike the others chosen, this one was not selected in advance. When I woke up this morning, in fact, I was wondering what I would put on this chapter's title page. In the last chapter, I shared the story of the much-needed outing with Dylan that inspired the discussion that served as its theme.

As happenstance, Noah and I went on a drive today just the two of us. Tomorrow, October 5, is his ninth birthday (Dylan turns 11 on October 7), so Noah wanted to run to Target to pick up a video game with some of his birthday money.

On the way there, I asked if he was game to visit a new nature preserve that I had wanted to try for a couple weeks, but because of some other commitments—the ones I am now grateful to have but promise not to be weighed down by—I hadn't had a chance to get there until today. It's called Fern Forest Nature Center in Coconut Creek. Paul, yes, Scrub-Jay Paul, works there and posted on the Broward birding group the place was hopping with warblers.

Considering he hadn't gone with me on a birding trip in a few weeks, Noah readily agreed, plus, like Dylan, he wanted some extra time with just me anyway. We showed up and met Paul, who was gracious to show us around.

We saw some familiar fall migrants I've already been fortunate, but still delighted, to see, including an Ovenbird, an American Redstart, and a Prairie Warbler—three of the birds that inspired the lessons and chapters in this book—while on a tour of a new undiscovered trail, the kind that always provides a sense of wonderment. We were led by Paul, a new friend, who has provided advice and guidance, and shared his knowledge for weeks but all online, until I met him for the first time today.

On our way to the parking lot, after thanking Paul for his help—not just for today but for everything over the last several weeks—I noticed some rustling in a nearby tree that, as it always does, made me stop and pause. It was a fall warbler I hadn't seen yet. It was not as rare as a Black-billed Cuckoo by any stretch, but not as common as, well, no need to name them. Let's just say, it was a balance. Right in the middle but it was new for me, one I'd never photographed before, and another new one for the "lifer" list.

It is a photo that will remind me of, not only the day I finished this book, but of the day that encapsulated so much of what I've come to appreciate about this endeavor over the last several months, wrapped into one outing.

One that fulfilled my sense of discovery and wonderment of the unknown.

One that provided a sense of adventure by exploring an unfamiliar place with a new peer lending his knowledge and sharing his wisdom.

One that included special one-on-one bonding time with one of my children that ended with the successful "mission" of spotting and photographing a new bird.

But, most of all, this photo will forever serve as the symbol for the parts of my journey that are yet to be determined, because when I woke up today, with this chapter already started, I still had no idea what would be on its title page.

Thus, the journey continues, and this beautiful Black-throated Blue Warbler will be here to remind me that it always will.

The End.

(but not really)

AFTERWORD

The Painted Bunting
December 2020

It's been two months since I finished this book. 2020 is wrapping up. I've seen a dozen or two new species over the last several weeks, including an incredibly rare-for-Florida female Western Tanager—yes, the same species of bird Jack Black identified by sound when bragging about this gift of his in *The Big Year* (a poignant and humorous tale on birding adapted from the book of the same name by Mark Obmascik). I moved up a few thousand spots on the eBird list. I met my friend, Ted, in person. I've been back to Walt Disney World. My oldest son, Dylan, has returned to the baseball field, and I've been back at work nearly three months. I've also been fortunate to be entertaining a family of Painted Buntings daily in my backyard, and that story serves as the final lesson of this book.

When I put my first feeder up in May—yes, the one I purchased after rejecting my mom's offer to buy me one not even a month earlier—attracting a Painted Bunting was the main reason why, knowing I'd need to wait a few months. In the meantime, to prepare and give myself the best odds, I decided to—based on research and recommendations from others, such as my friend, Ted—buy a caged feeder because I knew they could fit Buntings while keeping larger birds away, essentially making it safer and less intimidating for them to dine in peace. Instead of the generic grocery store brand of wild bird seed I had been using in my larger feeder, I ordered a special blend via Amazon that came recommended and now fills it.

Since I heard Buntings love white millet seed, I headed to Amazon once again, and yes, also ordered a third feeder that I filled with the millet. And, for good measure, it's the same feeder Ted uses to feed his own Bunting clan. Finally, as I shared earlier, a bird bath would help put the icing on the cake. These two new feeders and the bath are shown in the below collage.

By early September, my set-up was complete. Then it became time to wait. And wait. Fast forward to present day, mid-December, and for the past two months, I've enjoyed observing at least six Painted Buntings daily—male, female, and even some juveniles but here is the punchline, which is also represented in this collage. Where does the main male Painted Bunting visit most? You guessed it: the original large feeder I bought in May that continues to be filled with the generic grocery store brand seed. They will stop by all three feeders, but more often than not, when I look out back, the male is in his preferred spot, snacking away.

The point is this. Like so many things in life, birding and the rewards that come with it, can often come down to luck and a little bit of good fortune. For those more philosophical, you could say it comes down to "what's meant to be, will be." Either way, my Buntings came not because of the seed and feeders purchased but, I believe, because of something a little harder to quantify. Thus, the lesson here is that while it is always wise to put yourself in a position to find success, sometimes things have a way of working out how they're supposed to, regardless.

I chose to add this story as an afterword because it helps to underscore many of the lessons I shared in the previous pages. I was prepared, stayed positive, remained patient yet persistent, and never lost hope in the possibilities that someday I'd have a backyard full of these beautiful birds.

It is this pursuit of the elusive but attainable, and the ever-present optimism of good things being out there, that make birding—and, frankly, life in general— worth it.

ACKNOWLEDGEMENTS

I'd like to thank my family (Kristie, Dylan, Noah, and Emma); my parents (John and Ruth) and stepparents (or bonus parents as we call them! – Rick and Wendy); my grandparents (Lawrence, Wilma, Charles, and Stella); my siblings (John and Drew) and their spouses / my sisters-in-law (Billie and Samantha); my brother-in-law (Andrew) and his significant other (Megan); my in-laws (Linda and Jeff and Candace), and my nieces and nephews (Addy, Johnny, Sophia, Rylee, Jack, Smith, and Quincey). I'd like to also thank all my extended family members and friends, including those mentioned in the book as well as the coaches, teachers, bosses, and mentors noted throughout the preceding pages.

I'd like to thank Jackie Camacho-Ruiz and the entire team at Fig Factor Media, including Michele Kelly, Gaby Hernández Franch, Juan Pablo Ruiz, Manuel Serna and, Lisa Welz. It needs to be said I would not have been able to publish this book nor would I have been able to bring out its fullest potential without them! I would also like to recognize the authors and business leaders who took the time to provide tips and insights to me over the last few months, notably those who graciously offered to write words of praise for this book: Tim Kurkjian, Joseph Michelli, Leo Bottary, Hervé Humler, and Peter Kaestner.

To the Broward and South Florida birding community who welcomed a newbie with open arms, thank you for accepting me into the club! Lastly, I'd like to thank…the birds. All of them, from the Limpkin (my first photo taken on May 14, 2020) to the Scissor-tailed Fly Catcher (the most recent new observation made in March 2021, just as this book was nearing publication). To the Northern Cardinal, specifically (like the one on the cover of this book), as the bird who opened my eyes to the possibilities that are out there and reminds me of them to this day.

I am thankful, grateful, and blessed for each person (or bird!) who was with me every step of the way during this journey, both over the last 12 months as well as the last (nearly) 41 years of my life!

ABOUT THE AUTHOR

 **Matthew Papuchis** is an award-winning corporate communications strategist and internal communications leader and has worked for some of the world's leading brands and most admired companies, including Marriott International, The Ritz-Carlton Hotel Company, Carnival Cruise Line, and Sodexo, Inc.

Matt received his M.A. in Strategic Communication and Leadership from Seton Hall University and his B.S. in Mass Communication from Towson University, where he was the sports editor of the university newspaper, *The Towerlight*. Matt also has been a freelance journalist, with articles published in numerous publications including the *Washington Post*, *Baltimore Sun*, and the *Gazette* Newspapers of Montgomery County. He currently lives in Plantation, Florida and has three children (Dylan, Noah, and Emma).

CPSIA information can be obtained
at www.ICGtesting.com
Printed in the USA
LVHW081019170421
684786LV00002B/108